TRANS+

LOVE, SEX, ROMANCE, AND BEING YOU

BY
KATHRYN GONZALES, MBA
AND
KAREN RAYNE, PHD

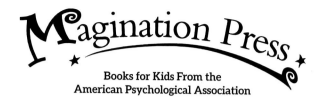

**Books for Kids From the
American Psychological Association**

Magination Press is a registered trademark of the American Psychological Association.

Order books at maginationpress.org, or call 1-800-374-2721.

Book design by Pam McElroy
Printed by Sonic Media Solutions, Inc., Medford, NY

Library of Congress Cataloging-in-Publication Data
Names: Gonzales, Kathryn, author. | Rayne, Karen, author.
Title: Trans+ : love, sex, romance, and being you / by Kathryn Gonzales, MBA and Karen Rayne, PhD.
Other titles: Trans plus
Description: Washington, DC : Magination Press, [2019] | Includes bibliographical references and index.
Identifiers: LCCN 2019007712| ISBN 9781433829833 (hardcover)| ISBN 1433829835 (hardcover)
Subjects: LCSH: Transgender people--Identity--Juvenile literature. | Gender nonconformity--Juvenile literature.
Classification: LCC HQ77.9 .R39 2019 | DDC 306.76/8--dc23
LC record available at https://lccn.loc.gov/2019007712

Manufactured in the United States of America
10 9 8 7 6 5 4 3 2 1

Contents

Life

Dear Reader,

No matter where you live, it is important to know this: Transgender and gender-nonbinary people have often held a revered place in their societies. We have been healers, shamans, revered rulers. We are no less than the stars and we are expressions of all that is beautiful in this universe that knows no other constant but change.

So go forward in this book, in your life, in your world, knowing that you are perfect, whole, and complete. Operate from a place where you know your own power, your own marvelousness.

Know that your ancestors were no less than gods.

Kathryn Gonzales, MBA   Karen Rayne, PhD

Welcome to *TRANS+*

The content in this book is honest, all-inclusive, uncensored, real-world information for teens who are transgender, nonbinary, gender-nonconforming, gender-fluid, or questioning their gender identity. *TRANS+* answers real questions about gender for real teens and covers mental health, physical health and reproduction, transitioning, relationships, sex, and life as a transgender or nonbinary individual. It's full of essential information you'll need to know and includes real-life stories from transgender and nonbinary teens.

Words

The language around gender is so important. There are a lot of words, from anatomy to psychology to culturally evolving words. If you don't know the definition of a word, don't let this intimidate you. Many of the chapters start with defining words that are important to that particular topic; and if you come across a word you don't know that isn't defined in the book, just do a quick internet search for it.

The language around gender, particularly as it applies to identity, is changing quickly. If there are words about identity that feel outdated, replace them with words that resonate for you.

Parents

When we talk about parents, we are referring to the people who raised you, whoever that means to you. Sometimes parents are biological and sometimes they're not. The parent–teen relationship is much more important than any kind of biological connection. So, if you have a different word or name that you use for your parents, we hope you'll think about them whenever we say parents. You can even take a pen and write in the person who is meaningful to you.

Authors' Notes

We included brief notes with our thoughts and feelings and personal connections to the chapter. We intend to use this opportunity to connect with you on another level and share our experiences as they relate to the chapter. We hope you enjoy our thoughts, musings, and occasional rants!

Additional Resources

At the end of each chapter are additional resources. These point to books, websites, blog posts, and more. Because the range of topics in this book is so large, some of the topics had so many additional resources that it was hard to narrow them down to just a few, while for other topics it was hard to find even one or two resources to recommend. But know that what we did include in these sections are some of the best resources available as of the writing of this book.

The Diary Entries

Each chapter includes diary entries written by trans and nonbinary youth and young adults. These diary entries are to show you how different youth relate to and live with the different topics every day. These are real people writing about their real experiences. Some of them are writing under their own name, some under a pen name.

These diary entries are one of the most profound and important parts of the book. We hope they move you as they moved us. There is something magical and transformative that happens in that first deep understanding that you are not alone in the world— that there are other people out there like you who are real.

To give you a sense of their personalities, the drawings of the authors show how they really look. Here are introductions to each of the authors in their own words:

Tai—I'm a transmasculine nonbinary person who has recently begun the process of social transition, publicly transitioning to male, and the time I spent questioning is crucial to my identity. In the past year, I've gone from identifying as a straight girl to an androsexual nonbinary individual to a pansexual demiboy. Currently, I identify as on the aromantic and asexual spectrums. As a person of color, intersectionality is dear to me and I consider it my mission make it more visible, accepted, and included.

Luka—I am a gay transgender man and I have been a part of the LGBT community for a very long time. My journey has been a long and tiring one, and it will continue to be so for a long time, but it has shaped me into the person I am today. My own identification journey as well as my interactions with other LGBT and non-LGBT people have shaped my perspective in a way that I do not often see presented among the community. I have identified on all sides of the gender and sexuality spectrum before understanding myself to be a gay man, and that, too, has shaped how I see things.

Johnny—I am a 16-year-old guy who really enjoys art and science. I have been undergoing medical transition for two years. I would, one day, like to be a medical examiner and I have a passion for English, music, visual art, and written art. I can usually be found going for runs or swinging on swing sets at my local neighborhood playground.

E.—I am a black, queer, nonbinary person, but those are not the only qualities that define me. I am intelligent, ambitious, creative, and strong. I like to think I'm funny, but those who know me might say otherwise. I am enormously flawed: simultaneously irrational and painfully rational. I love to learn, write, create, and dream. I start projects I know I will never finish in the hope I can make something of myself. I am a guitarist, a dancer, an artist, a designer, a student, a theatre technician, a debater, a club president, and the founder of the Central Texas GSA Coalition. Like everyone else on this Earth, I contain multitudes.

Drace—I am a 21-year-old computer engineering student currently living in Dallas, Texas. While I am an engineer by trade, I am a musician at heart who dreams of using my engineering skills to create all kinds of synthesizers and electronic instruments. As a transgender woman, I also want to help find opportunities for women and members of the LGBTQIA+ community in STEM-related fields. In my free time, I love listening to music, hanging out with friends, and DJing for anyone who will listen.

Danny—I am a transgender female-to-male (ftm); I come from a Catholic family, who are illegal immigrants. I didn't have the experience of saying I was a boy at the age of 2 because I didn't know what an LGBT person was in the first place. It was something I struggled with because I didn't know the label for it. I eventually learned what a transgender person is and it clicked. I want people to know that it isn't just about my family accepting me, but me learning and accepting myself.

End Matter

At the end of the book is a section with additional information, including a dictionary, chapter bibliography, and an index of the content in the entire book. These are great resources to refer to as you're reading the book or any time you hear something you'd like more information about.

INTRODUCTION

CHAPTER 1

WHAT IS GENDER?

Gender is hard because it is made up; it's a way that humans have developed over millennia to simplify how we see and interact with the world and the people in it. In reality, though, gender is complex and messy. The concept of gender has actually changed a lot over time, and not everyone agrees on the ways gender works or how others should embrace or embody their sense of gender.

Before we go any further in this book, it is important to make sure we understand each other and how we are going to talk about gender. Sharing a common language will help reduce misunderstandings. And, because the language of gender changes over time, the longer it is since we have published this book, the greater chance there is that some of these terms might feel a little dated.

As with everything in life, evaluate what is being presented to you through a critical lens. You are the one who gets to determine how you feel about gender and your relationship to it.

Sex vs. Gender

In many areas of your life, people will use the words "sex" and "gender" interchangeably. Sex is usually assigned to babies at birth based on the presence of specific genitalia. Gender is then assumed for the baby related to the sex they are assigned: babies assigned male at birth are thought of as "boys" and babies assigned female at birth are thought of as "girls."

For cisgender people (meaning people whose assigned sex at birth matches their gender identity), making the assumption of their gender at birth causes them few, if any, problems. But for transgender and nonbinary people (meaning people whose assigned sex at birth does not match their gender identity), making the assumption of their gender at birth can lead to a lifetime of challenges for them.

What About Intersex People?

Intersex[1] is a term used to describe a variety of conditions in which a person is born with reproductive organs or genitals that do not easily fit into the binary male/female construct of sex. This could mean that a baby is born with genitals that are larger or smaller than considered typical or with chromosomes that are not XX or XY. You will usually hear intersex people talked about in regards to their genitals, though sometimes the ways their bodies are different are not discovered until later in life or sometimes not ever.

Sadly, many parents and medical professionals are uncomfortable with intersex genitals and assign a binary sex to the baby anyway. They also often subject the baby to painful surgeries to "correct" what they deem is abnormal. And sometimes the sex they assign and do surgery to match doesn't actually match who the baby grows up to be, further complicating the baby's life.

Thankfully, advocates for intersex rights have raised awareness of these problems. In August 2018, the state of California became the first state to condemn "medically unnecessary surgeries" on intersex people. For more information about the intersex community and advocacy, check out interACT, a non-profit organization dedicated to protecting intersex youth.

---

1. The intersex community almost exclusively uses the term "intersex," however, you may hear the term "disorders of sex development" or "differences of sex development" in medical contexts. Because this medicalized terminology is controversial and pathologizing, you should avoid using it unless a person born with intersex traits identifies with its use.

So, What Is Gender?

Gender is a social construct that assigns people roles, tasks, responsibilities, and expected ways of being in the world based largely on the sex they were assigned at birth. Human beings are creatures that categorize and classify the world around them, so we boiled down gender to describe whether a person has a penis or doesn't have a penis—a simplified, and terribly inaccurate, binary classification system. This is what is meant when you hear the term "gender binary"—that there are only two choices and nothing in between: boy and girl, man and woman, masculine and feminine. And this binary has been and still is tightly controlled: "boys can't wear pink" or "girls can't play football."

Many people seek to control how gender is thought of and expressed because it gives them a false sense of control about the world around them and ensures they do not have to think too hard about all the ways humans exist. We should feel sorry for these people. Their binary thinking is so terribly limiting! Thankfully, we know better. We understand that gender is a spectrum and people can exist at any point along that spectrum (or entirely outside of it) at any given moment of their life.

I like dresses, but only sometimes, and only on my own terms. What does that mean? I've always fit in with the boys more, and I understand them better than I understand girls, but is that enough to make me one of them? I hate when people say, "Ladies first," to me, but is that because I don't like being gendered that way, or I just don't like the special treatment? I don't wear makeup or like cute things because that would make me seem like a girl, but I would want to see cis men doing those things if they wanted to...

I have a lot of friends from very different backgrounds, and they want to understand me but have no concept of the kind of questioning and self-doubt I put myself through every day. People will ask me why I feel like I'm a boy, why I can't be a girl, why I have to make such a big deal about going to the bathroom (I complained to my brother once about it being difficult to find a bathroom that I can use safely, and his only response was that I chose that struggle). I know they're just trying to genuinely understand me and my experience, so I'll try my best to answer them, but for every answer there's a counterexample. They tell me I could just be a tomboy, they tell me my body looks good and I shouldn't change it, they tell me I'm good just the way I am, they ask why can't I just be "myself" and ignore the things I don't like, they tell me that I'm no different from anyone else.

After hours of talking in circles, asking all kinds of questions, shooting all kinds of theories, it always ends the same way. If gender doesn't have to be related to sex, to clothing, to interests, to personality, to sexual orientation, to presentation—then what is gender?

Tai

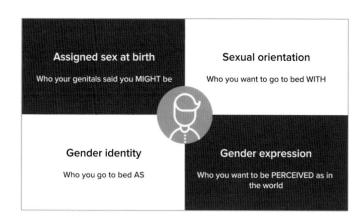

Assigned sex at birth	Sexual orientation
Who your genitals said you MIGHT be	Who you want to go to bed WITH
Gender identity	Gender expression
Who you go to bed AS	Who you want to be PERCEIVED as in the world

Are We Saying the Same Thing?

Before we dive deeper into how people identify their gender, let's make sure we are using words about gender in the same way.

- **Gender identity** is a person's internal sense of who they know themselves to be at their core, regardless of what other people think or say. It captures how they relate or do not relate to the social constructs that their culture aligns with the sex they were assigned at birth. A person's gender identity is not something that they choose.

- **Gender expression** encompasses all the ways that a person shows their gender to the world around them. This information can be conveyed through a person's hair, clothes, make-up, mannerisms, etc. Each person gets to choose how they express their gender. When the choice is to express a gender that isn't authentic though, it can be really hard on that person psychologically.

- **Biological sex** encompasses the complex group of physical factors that are assigned to male, female, and intersex. Biological sex is usually determined by a combination of anatomical and genetic factors. A person's biological sex is not something that they choose.

- **Sexual attraction** is the feeling of physical connection, desire, and arousal. Sometimes people do not experience sexual attraction. How a person experiences sexual attraction is not something that they choose.

- **Romantic attraction** describes the desire for a certain type of relationship with another person that involves emotional closeness and caring for each other in an intimate, fulfilling, and supportive way. Sometimes people do not experience romantic attraction. How a person experiences romantic attraction is not something that they choose.

- **AMAB (assigned male at birth)** is a term used to describe a person who was assumed to be male when they were born because they had a penis. A person does not choose to be AMAB; this choice is made for them.

- **AFAB (assigned female at birth)** is a term used to describe a person who was assumed to be female when they were born because they had a vulva. A person does not choose to be AFAB; this choice is made for them.

All the Colors of the Rainbow

We talk a lot about gender identity, gender expression, sexual attraction, and romantic attraction being spectrums. You may have even seen older models of identity that place male/masculinity at one end and female/femininity at the other and invite you to place yourself somewhere along that spectrum. The problem is, that just enforces the gender binary and we want to disrupt it.

There is another way of thinking about these concepts with each of them on their own spectra. This allows for a person to be, for example, high in both masculinity *and* femininity. Or low in both. It allows for so much more freedom of understanding and expression! On the next page is an example of how that can look. (There are other ways to do this, the one included here is just one possibility.)

We love this new way of thinking about how people identify. Yes, it still uses a binary frame to an extent (sometimes you have to work from within the system to dismantle it), but this new way of depicting identity allows for different levels of both binary concepts—or rejecting them altogether.

The most important thing to remember is that these ways of identifying yourself can (and most likely will) change over time. This does not mean you or anyone else can intentionally change your gender identity or sexual orientation. It also does not mean you were wrong before or that you were lying to the people around you. It just means that as you grow and learn more about yourself, you have become increasingly skillful at knowing who you are and how you exist in the world at each point in time.

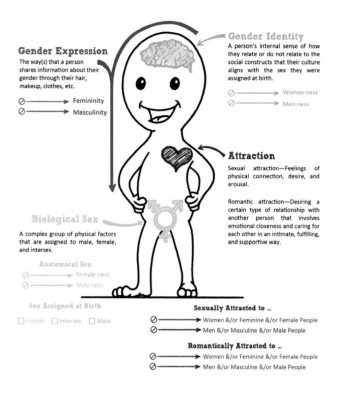

Gender Expression
The way(s) that a person shares information about their gender through their hair, makeup, clothes, etc.

⊘—————▶ Femininity
⊘—————▶ Masculinity

Gender Identity
A person's internal sense of how they relate or do not relate to the social constructs that their culture aligns with the sex they were assigned at birth.

⊘—————▶ Woman-ness
⊘—————▶ Man-ness

Attraction
Sexual attraction—Feelings of physical connection, desire, and arousal.

Romantic attraction—Desiring a certain type of relationship with another person that involves emotional closeness and caring for each other in an intimate, fulfilling, and supportive way.

Biological Sex
A complex group of physical factors that are assigned to male, female, and intersex.

Anatomical Sex
⊘—————▶ Female-ness
⊘—————▶ Male-ness

Sex Assigned at Birth
☐ Female ☐ Intersex ☐ Male

Sexually Attracted to …
⊘—————▶ Women &/or Feminine &/or Female People
⊘—————▶ Men &/or Masculine &/or Male People

Romantically Attracted to …
⊘—————▶ Women &/or Feminine &/or Female People
⊘—————▶ Men &/or Masculine &/or Male People

Gender Around the World and Over Time

We are writing this book from a Western 21st-century point of view, and, as such, most of this book will speak to that same point of view.

But gender is not universal. It has and continues to show up in all kinds of different ways around the world. In some cultures and countries, the enforcement of the gender binary is quite strict, often limiting the self-expression, movement, and autonomy of people perceived to be female. In other cultures, there are more than two recognized genders, in some cases, there are five or more! And in some places, the binary is breaking down altogether.

On the following pages is just a sampling of the kinds of gender variance that have been and may continue to be found around the world. This information is important for you to know so you can understand you are not alone. Gender variance is found all over the world and throughout human history. We can be found everywhere and in every time period.

The Western "Third Gender"

"Third Gender" is used by Western anthropologists as an umbrella term to describe all kinds of gender variant identities. This term is super muddy, though. Some anthropologists use it for every kind of gender identity that isn't cisgender. Others use it only to describe people who might be considered transgender women. And others use it not to describe gender variance as we've been talking about it—they use it to describe cisgender LGB people. *We know, we know.* We already defined the differences between gender identity and sexual orientation a few sections back, but in fairness, we don't think any of these anthropologists have read our book.

Gender is a very complex phenomenon. No, I personally don't believe gender is necessarily a social construct, but it's definitely psychological. There are many different ways people determine gender, and it's often predetermined or assigned at birth. However, gender isn't synonymous with sex.

I don't feel that gender is a "social construct" like some people say. Gender is defined on dictionary.com as "either the male or female division of a species, especially as differentiated by social and cultural roles and behavior." What does that mean to me? Why did I choose to tell you the definition? Gender isn't a matter of choice. Gender is psychologically coded into your brain. Though gender is coded into our brains, it might not always match what our body's biological sex may be. An example of gender could also be when someone says "are you a boy or a girl?" and you feel a strong need to answer "boy" when your doctor assigned you "girl" at birth, or vice versa.

I often wonder: Why am I trans? When exactly did I realize I was different? And other complicated gender questions. I then find myself researching and reading different biological theories and psychological studies about what could influence my gender, like if I was overexposed to a certain hormone or if it was just a freak accident. I've read many studies and one even did experiments on rats inutero to see if what hormones they were introduced to affected how and what they grew up to be. There are also studies about chromosomes and genes, and how we could be born with a mismatched set of them or with a few extras that make only a small difference.

No matter if it's a social construct, psychological, hormonal, or predetermined at birth, gender is a really hard and difficult thing to understand and recognize about yourself.

Johnny

Africa

- **Ashtime** is a term used by the Maale people in Ethiopia to describe AMAB eunuchs (an AMAB person who has had their testicles removed) who live as women.

- **Mino** was a term used in Benin (Kingdom of Dahomey, 1600-1904 AD) to describe AFAB warriors who were perceived to be more masculine than other AFAB people.

- **Sekhet** was a term used in ancient Egypt (Middle Kingdom, 2000-1800 BCE) to describe one of the three genders: men, sekhet, and women, in that order (probably to indicate that sekhet was in-between the two binary genders). This term is usually translated as eunuch, but it could have also been used to describe cisgender gay men.

- **Sekrata** is a term used by the Sakalava people in Madagascar to describe transgender women.

Americas

- **Dilbaa** is a term used by the Navajo to describe AFAB people who have a masculine gender role.

- **Muxe** is a term used by the Zapotec people in Mexico to describe AMAB people who have a feminine gender expression.

- **Nadleehi** is a term used by the Navajo to describe AMAB people who have a feminine gender role.

- **Ninauposkitzipxpe** is a term used by the Blackfoot Confederacy and translates to "manly hearted women"—AFAB people who have a gender role that is different from cisgender men and women.

- **Quariwarmi** was a term used by the Incas in Peru (prior to Spanish colonization and the fall of the Incan empire in 1572) to describe a nonbinary gender role.

- **Two-spirit** is a term used internationally to describe the gender roles and identities adopted by hundreds of cultures in North and South America.

- **Winkte** is a term used by the Lakota to describe AMAB people who have a gender role similar to cisgender women.

Asia & Middle East

- **Acault** is a term used in Myanmar to describe AMAB people with a feminine gender expression.

- **Bacah posh** is a term used in Afghanistan and Pakistan to describe an AFAB child in a family with no sons who is raised as a male or intermediate gender role. When the child grows up, they are pressured to switch back to a female gender role so they can get married.

- **Hijra** is a term used in South Asian countries to describe AMAB people with a feminine gender expression. Hijra are legally recognized as their own gender.

- **Kathoey** is a term used in Thailand to describe transgender women or feminine gay men.

- **Köçek** was a term used in Turkey (Ottoman Empire, 17th century) to describe AMAB people with a feminine gender expression.

- **Metis** is a term used in Nepal to describe AMAB people with a feminine gender expression.

Kathryn

Writing this section made me cry. I have always felt so lonely as a trans woman. Yes, I have many trans and nonbinary friends, I work at an LGBTQIA+ youth center, and I volunteer for various LGBTQIA+ causes, and still, I've felt lonely. To research and write about the history of our people, to know at a deeper level that we have always existed throughout human history, made me feel less alone. It's as if I could hear the voice of our ancestors urging me forward, so that you may know that you aren't alone either.

- **Mukhannathun** (مخنّثون) is a term used in classical Arabic writings to describe transgender women or very feminine gay men.

- **Waria** is a term used in Indonesia to describe a third gender.

- **X-gender** (Xジェンダー) is a term used in Japan to describe a transgender identity.

- **Xanith** is a term used in Oman to describe AMAB people with a partially feminine gender expression.

- **Yinyang ren** is a term used in China to describe people who have equal proportions of feminine (yin) and masculine (yang) characteristics. This term is usually used to describe gender-nonbinary people and bisexuals but can also be used to describe transgender or intersex people.

Australia & Oceania

- **Akava'ine** is a term used in the Cook Islands to describe people who do not fit into the gender binary.

- **Brotherboy** is a term used in Australia, Queensland Aboriginal, and Torres Strait Islander communities to describe transgender men.

The Five Genders of the Bugis People

Many cultures have specific words for gender identities. What makes the Bugis people of Indonesia exceptional is that they not only recognize five different gender identities, they believe all five must coexist in harmony for a society to function.

- **Bissu** is the term for people who may or may not be intersex and combine all genders.
- **Calabai** is the term for transgender women.
- **Calalai** is the term for transgender men.
- **Makkunrai** is the term for cisgender women.
- **Oroané** is the term for cisgender men.

- **Fa'afafine** is a term used in Samoa to describe AMAB people with a feminine gender expression and who do not identify as female or male.

- **Mahu** is a term used by the Kanaka Maoli people of Hawaii (prior to and survived through Western colonization) to describe a nonbinary gender role.

- **Sistergirl** is a term used in Australia, Queensland Aboriginal, and Torres Strait Islander communities to describe transgender women.

- **Wakatane** is a term used by the Maori people in New Zealand to describe AFAB people with a masculine gender expression.

- **Whakawahine** is a term used by the Maori people in New Zealand to describe AMAB people with a feminine gender expression.

Europe

- **Burrnesha** (or "sworn virgins") is a term that has been used in Albania since the 1400s to describe AFAB people with a masculine gender expression.

Gender isn't something that can be easily defined and, to be honest, I'm still not sure what the word means to me. Before I began my transition, gender felt like a set of expectations others had for me because of how I was born, and it was used as a way for people to assume things about my personality before ever getting to know me. I always hated that feeling and, to this day, it still brings me discomfort. Now that I am a lot further in the transition process my gender feels more reassuring and comfortable, almost like a warm blanket on a cold day. I feel as though people's assumptions of me are a little more accurate now than they were before, but sometimes I still feel like I'm being unfairly judged because of my gender. Even though being feminine brings me so much comfort, I still hate the idea of people thinking they know something about me just because of the way I present myself. It's such a tricky feeling to deal with, feeling so held back by gender, yet also feeling like it has set me free. If gender is something that is going to play a role in my life, I want it to benefit me, not push me down. I think that's ultimately why I transitioned in the first place, because I don't want my gender to be something that defines me; I want my gender to let me define myself. I know who I am, I always have, but the hard part is trying to get other people on the same page. For now, though, I can't keep worrying how other people perceive me. For now, my gender is giving me the confidence I need to live my life to the fullest and, as long as I feel I am being true to myself, I shouldn't dwell on what other people think.

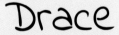

Drace

- **Femminello** (or "little man woman") is a term used in Italy to describe AMAB people with a feminine gender expression.

- **Gallae** is a term that originated in Turkey and spread across Europe to describe the ancient priestesses of the goddess Cybele who were AMAB eunuchs.

You Are Not Alone

Now that you've seen the many ways people who fit outside of the Western gender binary identify, and now that we're on the same page about the meaning of some key terms and concepts, we hope you feel a little more confident and a little less alone. Not only are you not alone, but you are also part of a strong, important global history.

Even so, the process of figuring out your gender can be hard, confusing, and isolating. So, do us a favor? When you are feeling especially lonely, return to this chapter. Read about all the beautiful trans and nonbinary people around the world and throughout history. Remind yourself that transgender and gender-nonbinary people have always existed and will continue to exist far into the future.

I have always felt . . . off. For a while, I was able to explain away my issues with a quick, easy "I'm not like other girls." But that stopped working and I didn't know why. I didn't like who I was, but it wasn't until recently that I attributed any of my feelings to gender—I don't even think I had a conception of what gender was. I don't remember if there was an "aha" moment, and maybe it just hasn't happened yet, but the gradual expansion of my knowledge of the fluid nature of genders has helped me realize the source of my insecurity, though it feels like no amount of information in the world could help me solve it.

This internal struggle has continued for what seems like forever. I still don't know who I am, and I don't know if it matters. How do I reconcile my internal turmoil with society's neurotic need to categorize everything? I know I don't fit into the box they have carelessly thrown me into; I cringe when people call me a girl. I am floating in a void surrounded by thousands of boxes, all different shapes and sizes, some labeled and some not, unsure which is for me. Am I androgynous, gender-fluid, nonbinary, transmasculine, genderqueer, bigender, agender, or anything in between? And how will I know when I've found what fits?

In a society that values simplicity, the complexity of gender is far from being embraced. Our nuanced differences are part of what makes us human, and I hope we can learn to accept and celebrate them, no matter what those differences may be.

E.

Additional Resources

For more conversations and thoughts about gender, here are a few resources:

 thetransbook.com/link/0101
This is the website for the amazing global radical body acceptance movement, The Body Is Not an Apology. All kinds of gender issues are covered, as well as issues pertaining to weight/size, disability, sexuality, mental health, race, and aging.

thetransbook.com/link/0102
This video was created by youth for youth and uses incredible animations to explain the core concepts of gender.

thetransbook.com/link/0103
InterACT is a phenomenal organization that advocates for the rights of intersex youth and adults.

CHAPTER 2

GENDER DYSPHORIA

Gender may be imaginary, but gender dysphoria is not. Caused by the mismatch between assigned sex/gender at birth and a person's understanding of their own identity, gender dysphoria can range from a minor annoyance to a source of significant emotional and mental distress.

In this chapter, we explore the different ways dysphoria can show up, body image, strategies for managing feelings of dysphoria, and how dysphoria is sometimes used by mental health and medical providers to determine a person's readiness for medical transition.

What Is Gender Dysphoria?

Gender dysphoria is a feeling of discomfort brought on by a person's sex assigned to them at birth not matching the gender they know themselves to be.

This feeling of discomfort can show up in many ways. Here are five of them:

- **Body dysphoria** is a sense of discomfort about aspects of a person's body that do not match how they understand and seek to express their gender.

- **Genital dysphoria** is a sense of discomfort caused when a person's genitals do not match their gender identity.

- **Mental dysphoria** is a sense of discomfort caused when a person's thoughts and emotions don't match their gender identity.

- **Sexual dysphoria** is a sense of discomfort while having sex that is caused by a combination of body and genital dysphoria, as well as how a person's sexual partner(s) see, talk about, and interact with their body.

- **Social dysphoria** is a sense of discomfort brought on in social situations due to assumptions made about a person's gender. This can be brought on by misgendering (when someone uses the wrong gender pronouns) and deadnaming (when someone uses a person's old name) as well as other verbal and non-verbal cues.

Some people experience all of these kinds of dysphoria, while others only experience one or two kinds. Be gentle with yourself when you are experiencing these feelings. They can be hard to manage internally and it can be hard to figure out how to talk to other people about them. It's also important to know that your feelings of dysphoria will likely change over time.

Managing Feelings of Dysphoria

Dysphoria can make you feel everything from mildly annoyed to suicidal and everything in between. That's why it's important to find ways to deal with the dysphoria when it comes up. If you don't deal with it in healthy ways, your annoyed feelings can cause you to lash out at yourself or at other people. The suicidal feelings can cause everything from depression to self-harm. But it doesn't have to be that way. There are better, healthier ways to manage dysphoria.

The best approach is to find a therapist who specializes in working with transgender and gender-nonbinary youth. Therapists who understand what you're going through; who have a whole bunch of information and tools that are designed for trans and nonbinary youth; and who know how to talk with your parents, school, and other people in your life can be a huge source of support. You can often find a therapist by contacting your local LGBTQ+ center or LGBTQ+ youth program. And if you don't live near an LGBTQ+ center, some therapists offer teletherapy where you have your sessions by video chat or phone.

What if your parents are resistant to the idea of therapy, or simply don't want you talking to someone who will validate your identity? Try asking a trusted adult, family member, or friend to talk to your parents and express why they think therapy is a good idea for you. While we don't like it to be this way, sometimes parents are able to hear suggestions and understand why they're important from another adult. If therapy is just out of the question, you can talk to these same trusted adults, family members, and friends about what you're going through.

If you're not ready to talk to a therapist or other trusted adult, you can turn to other transgender and gender-nonbinary youth online to talk about what you're experiencing. Often times, youth will turn to websites like YouTube and Tumblr to learn more about their identities and hear stories about other people's transitions. Commenting and engaging in these communities can provide good support and even point you to other online groups for help.

Finding ways to express your gender that feel authentic can help as well. You might experiment with different clothes, try different mannerisms, change your voice, and other ways of signaling your gender. We know that you might have some questions about how to do some of these things, which we cover in Chapter 7.

You might also try using a creative outlet like writing, drawing, or music to capture and process your feelings. If you're comfortable, you can share these creations with other transgender and gender-nonbinary youth so they know they're not alone.

There's no right way to do any of this. But if things get so bad that you think of hurting yourself, definitely talk with someone. The Trevor Project is a good place to start.

Karen

People who aren't trans don't understand gender dysphoria. But they should—if they are kind and compassionate people—listen to you share your experiences as and when you are able. Your friends and family not having the experience is no reason for them to not do the emotional labor of being supportive and loving you and taking your needs into account.

I have two devils on my shoulders. The one on the left wishes my hair was shorter, my jaw was more prominent, my chest was flatter, and my muscles were more defined. It wishes I didn't look so feminine. The one on the right wishes my hair was smoother, my skin was clearer, my curves were curvier, my stomach was flatter. It wishes I looked prettier. These devils keep fighting and tearing me apart, because as soon as I fulfill one's wishes, the other emerges with a vengeance.

This is what dysphoria is like for me. A constant conflict between what I want to be and what society wants me to be. The cheering supporters of the devil on the right are never enough to drown out the haunting whispers of the devil on the left.

Every day, I do my makeup—foundation, contour, highlight, eyebrows, eyeliner, mascara, lip gloss—hoping I can suffocate my insecurities in layer after layer of cakey product. Despite my goal of masculinity, I can never seem to bring myself to forego the makeup. I think a lot of my dysphoria is a result of how society perceives me. I want to be able to pass as male, but no matter how hard I try, people always seem to just see me as an ugly girl, not as anything close to a boy or an androgynous person, so to combat my self-hatred, I end up presenting very feminine.

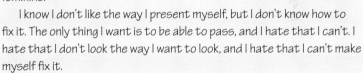

I know I don't like the way I present myself, but I don't know how to fix it. The only thing I want is to be able to pass, and I hate that I can't. I hate that I don't look the way I want to look, and I hate that I can't make myself fix it.

E.

Dysphoria and Who Gets to Decide: Gatekeeper vs. Informed Consent

When it comes to medical transition (whether that means hormone replacement therapy[1], surgery, or other procedures), there are two ways to decide who gets to make the decision if these treatments should start. In the *gatekeeper model*, a therapist decides if a person is "trans enough" and "ready" for medical transition. This is often tied to the person's feelings of dysphoria. This is one of those very upsetting examples of when (mostly) cisgender people decide that a certain way of doing something is best for transgender people, even though it doesn't make a lot of sense and may actually be harmful. In the *informed consent model*, the decision to start medical transition is made by the transgender or gender-nonbinary person after they've talked with their doctor and understand the pros and cons of the treatments they want.

The Gatekeeper Model

In the gatekeeper model, transgender and gender-nonbinary people are required to go to therapy—in some cases for several months—to receive a letter from their therapist giving them a diagnosis of gender dysphoria.

But here's the thing: being transgender or gender-nonbinary is not a mental health disorder. Unfortunately, in many parts of the world, it is still necessary to seek a mental health diagnosis of "gender dysphoria" (or the now-outdated diagnostic term "gender identity disorder") before you can begin any kind of medical transition.

The problem with the requirement to obtain a diagnosis is that it asks transgender and gender-nonbinary people to repeatedly prove their "transness" to receive the medical care they require or desire, which, in many cases, causes more dysphoria. This gatekeeping approach (think of a person standing at a gate and deciding who can go in and who can't) has arisen due to transphobia. Specifically, the unwillingness to believe that person is who they say they are, as well as insurance companies' unwillingness to pay for transition-related health care, is why the gatekeeping model is a thing.

---

1 For some people, the phrase "hormone replacement therapy" is triggering because it refers to their need to "replace" their original hormonal make-up. Some people prefer the phrase "hormone therapy." You get to decide which phrase is best for you.

To make a diagnosis of gender dysphoria, a medical or mental health professional will use one of two classification systems. It's important for you to understand both systems and their requirements, even if we don't agree with their use (we prefer the informed consent model, which we describe later on in this chapter), in case you are asked to prove that you are transgender or gender-nonbinary.

The Diagnostic Statistical Manual of Mental Disorders (DSM) has two sets of criteria for diagnosing gender dysphoria: one for children and another for adolescents (a fancy word for teenagers) and adults.

The thing that's weird about these two sets of diagnostic criteria is the number of minimum criteria a person has to meet to be diagnosed with gender dysphoria. For children, they have to meet *six* of the eight criteria while adolescents and adults only have to meet *two* of the six criteria. This just reinforces the belief that children are "too young" to know what their gender is.

Kathryn

In the fifth edition of the Diagnostic Statistical Manual of Mental Disorders (DSM–5), the outdated term "gender identity disorder" was replaced with the term "gender dysphoria." While I don't like that gender dysphoria is still considered a mental health diagnosis, the removal of the word "disorder" was a step in the right direction.

Diagnostic Statistical Manual of Mental Disorders (DSM-5)

Gender Dysphoria in Children | 302.6 (F64.2)

A. A marked incongruence between one's experienced/expressed gender and assigned gender, of at least 6 months' duration, as manifested by at least six of the following (one of which must be Criterion A1):

1. A strong desire to be of the other gender or an insistence that one is the other gender (or some alternative gender different from one's assigned gender).

2. In boys (assigned gender), a strong preference for cross-dressing or simulating female attire: or in girls (assigned gender), a strong preference for wearing only typical masculine clothing and a strong resistance to the wearing of typical feminine clothing.

3. A strong preference for cross-gender roles in make-believe play or fantasy play.

4. A strong preference for the toys, games, or activities stereotypically used or engaged in by the other gender.

5. A strong preference for playmates of the other gender.

6. In boys (assigned gender), a strong rejection of typically masculine toys, games, and activities and a strong avoidance of rough-and-tumble play; or in girls (as signed gender), a strong rejection of typically feminine toys, games, and activities.

7. A strong dislike of one's sexual anatomy.

8. A strong desire for the primary and/or secondary sex characteristics that match one's experienced gender.

B. The condition is associated with clinically significant distress or impairment in social, school, or other important areas of functioning.

Gender Dysphoria in Adolescents and Adults | 302.85 (F64.1)

A. A marked incongruence between one's experienced/expressed gender and assigned gender, of at least 6 months' duration, as manifested by at least two of the following:

1. A marked incongruence between one's experienced/expressed gender and primary and/or secondary sex characteristics (or in young adolescents, the anticipated secondary sex characteristics).

2. A strong desire to be rid of one's primary and/or secondary sex characteristics because of a marked incongruence with

one's experienced/expressed gender (or in young adolescents, a desire to prevent the development of the anticipated secondary sex characteristics).

3. A strong desire for the primary and/or secondary sex characteristics of the other gender.
4. A strong desire to be of the other gender (or some alternative gender different from one's assigned gender).
5. A strong desire to be treated as the other gender (or some alternative gender different from one's assigned gender).
6. A strong conviction that one has the typical feelings and reactions of the other gender (or some alternative gender different from one's assigned gender).

B. The condition is associated with clinically significant distress or impairment in social, occupational, or other important areas of functioning.

From *Diagnostic and statistical manual of mental disorders, fifth edition*, by American Psychiatric Association. Copyright 2013 by author. Reprinted with permission.

Kathryn

The DSM–5 criteria for diagnosing someone with gender dysphoria is all over the trans-inclusive map. In some cases, they use phrases like "a gender different than the one assigned to them at birth" which is generally felt to be inclusive. Then there are references to "feminine" or "masculine" clothing and toys which makes us wonder how those using the DSM might define "feminine clothing" or "masculine toys." It is important to note that the DSM includes these terms in quotation marks, indicating that the authors understand these words to carry meaning that should be treated with care, but don't go so far as to clearly state how they believe these words should be treated in practice. The criteria that concerns us most is the one asserting that "a strong dislike of their genitals" is a valid indicator of gender dysphoria in children, but the same is not true for adolescents and adults.

The International Classification of Diseases (IDC-10)

F64.0 Transexualism

A desire to live and be accepted as a member of the opposite sex, usually accompanied by a sense of discomfort with, or inappropriateness of, one's anatomic sex, and a wish to have surgery and hormonal treatment to make one's body as congruent as possible with one's preferred sex.

F64.2 Gender Identity Disorder of Childhood

A disorder, usually first manifested during early childhood (and always well before puberty), characterized by a persistent and intense distress about assigned sex, together with a desire to be (or insistence that one is) of the other sex. There is a persistent preoccupation with the dress and activities of the opposite sex and repudiation of the individual's own sex. The diagnosis requires a profound disturbance of the normal gender identity; mere tomboyishness in girls or girlish behaviour in boys is not sufficient. Gender identity disorders in individuals who have reached or are entering puberty should not be classified here but in F66.

F66.0 Sexual Maturation Disorder

The patient suffers from uncertainty about his or her gender identity or sexual orientation, which causes anxiety or depression. Most commonly this occurs in adolescents who are not certain whether they are homosexual, heterosexual or bisexual in orientation, or in individuals who, after a period of apparently stable sexual orientation (often within a longstanding relationship), find that their sexual orientation is changing.

From "The ICD–10 classification of mental and behavioural disorders" by World Health Organization, retrieved from https://www.who.int/classifications/icd/en/bluebook.pdf. Copyright 1993 by author. Reprinted with permission.

The International Classification of Diseases (IDC-11)

HA60 Gender Incongruence of Adolescence or Adulthood

Gender Incongruence of Adolescence and Adulthood is characterized by a marked and persistent incongruence between an individual's experienced gender and the assigned sex, which often leads to a desire to 'transition', in order to live and be accepted as a person of the experienced gender, through hormonal treatment, surgery or other health care services to make the individual's body align, as much as desired and to the extent possible with the experienced gender. The diagnosis cannot be assigned prior the onset of puberty. Gender variant behaviour and preferences alone are not a basis for assigning the diagnosis.

HA61 Gender Incongruence of Childhood

Gender incongruence of childhood is characterized by a marked incongruence between an individual's experienced/expressed gender and the assigned sex in pre-pubertal children. It includes a strong desire to be a different gender than the assigned sex; a strong dislike on the child's part of his or her sexual anatomy or anticipated secondary sex characteristics and/or a strong desire for the primary and/or anticipated secondary sex characteristics that match the experienced gender; and make-believe or fantasy play, toys, games, or activities and playmates that are typical of the experienced gender rather than the assigned sex. The incongruence must have persisted for about 2 years. Gender variant behaviour and preferences alone are not a basis for assigning the diagnosis.

Kathryn

It is fascinating to look at the drastic improvement in language used between the ICD-10 and ICD-11.

The ICD-10 uses problematic phrases like "opposite sex," "preferred sex," "normal gender identity," and "disorder." It also asserts that a "wish to have surgery and hormonal treatment" is necessary to validate a person's transgender identity. Worst of all, the ICD-10 criteria refers to section F66 if the person is a teenager, which mentions gender identity only in passing (and after using the gendered "his or her"), and then gives an example that only speaks to a changing sexual orientation that further conflates sexual orientation and gender identity.

The ICD-11 takes a much more inclusive approach to talking about gender identity, specifically calling out the "incongruence" that a person experiences between their assigned sex and their actual lived experience of their gender. It also addresses the possibility that a person may seek "hormonal treatment, surgery or other health care services" but only "as much as desired or to the extent possible." This reinforces the belief that it should be the trans person making decisions about their body and transition. The ICD-11 isn't perfect though, especially when talking about trans kids. It still implies a gender binary when insinuating that there is a "typical" experienced gender for children and sets minimum 2-year time persistence requirement that seems arbitrary without further explanation.

The Informed Consent Model

The alternative to the gatekeeping approach is called "informed consent." In the informed consent model, medical providers explain the risks and benefits of a chosen treatment and, once informed, the patient can choose whether or not they consent to the treatment.

Informed consent isn't a new concept created to make it easier for transgender and gender-nonbinary people to get the treatment they need or desire. In some cases, transgender people are required to jump through hoops to get necessary medical treatments related to their gender identity when the same treatments are used to address other medical issues relatively easily. For example, the drug Spironolactone can be used to treat high blood

Criteria for the Informed Consent Model

This is where the criteria for the informed consent model would go if there were any. But there isn't a single, unified approach to informed consent. That's because doctors and patients have been doing health care by informed consent for centuries.

Under the informed consent model, a doctor who feels comfortable will (without requiring that person to get assessed and diagnosed by a therapist first):

- assess the person seeking treatment;
- make a diagnosis of gender dysphoria; and
- assess the person's ability to provide their informed consent for treatment, meaning that they understand all of the
  - risks of treatment,
  - benefits of treatment,
  - alternatives to treatment,
  - unknowns of treatment,
  - limitations of treatment, and
  - risks of not getting treatment.

Once someone gives informed consent, their doctor will start them on hormone replacement therapy and other medical interventions as needed.

Because a teenager in the United States who is not yet 18 cannot give legal consent, that young person's parent would be the one giving the informed consent. When they turn 18, the young person can begin to give their own informed consent. The age at which a person can give their own informed consent varies from country to country.

pressure, but it also happens to be an androgen blocker that can be used as part of a feminizing hormone treatment. If medicine wasn't practiced using informed consent, a person going to the doctor for Spironolactone would first have to see a therapist to make sure it was believable that the person both had high blood pressure and understood the risks of the medication. We don't know about you, but that sounds silly to us. Thankfully, medicine is usually practiced using informed consent, meaning that a person going to the doctor for Spironolactone to treat high blood pressure would be assessed, talk to their doctor about the benefits and risks of taking the drug, and then decide if they want to go ahead with treatment. We look forward to the day when being transgender is treated with the same respect and appropriate medical interventions as other medical issues.

Feelings and Processes

Dysphoria sucks. One minute you can be having an amazing day, and the next someone misgenders you and dysphoria kicks your butt. The best that you can do in those moments is recognize that other people's perceptions of your gender do not change who you already know yourself to be.

Dysphoria is a feeling that comes as part of a larger process of coming to know yourself and, when you're ready, telling others. Sometimes your dysphoria is going to be worse than other times. Maybe your friends are super supportive so you feel less dysphoric with them than you do when you visit your grandparents who have a hard time with your new name and pronouns.

When your dysphoria gets really bad, do something that connects and grounds you to your identity. You can journal about the feelings you experience or play a video game that allows you to become a character that reflects your gender identity. Whatever it is, take time to be gentle with yourself.

Dysphoria is a hard concept to deal with, and it can hold a lot of people back from living their lives to the fullest. Even now, after being out for two and a half years and starting HRT almost two years ago, I still experience dysphoria fairly frequently. Whether it's noticing the size of my shoulders, or realizing I'm taller than most of the people around me, it can be a major blow to my confidence. I know people always say "you are your own worst critic," but it can be hard not to internalize these uncomfortable feelings, and it can really affect your self-esteem. The one thing I've noticed, though, since I began to transition, is that no matter how far along you are in the transition process, it only gets easier. Regardless of how I'm currently feeling about my body, I can always look at old pictures of myself and realize how far I've come. I can see how I went from an insecure teenager uncomfortable with my gender to a more confident young adult still determined to improve myself to be the best I can be. Two years ago I would have thought it impossible to be where I am now, and I know in two more years I will be in a place I think would be impossible now. Maybe I will have a new wardrobe, maybe I will get a little better at makeup, or maybe I'll even get the gender affirming surgeries I've been wanting since I began transitioning. Regardless of the form my progress takes, I know I will continue to love myself even more as time passes, and even though I have rough days often, I know things will get better, and no one can stop me from being the best me I can be.

Drace

Dysphoria makes me feel shameful. I feel as if I look like some sort of thing that is between a woman and a man. There are days where I don't want to go out because I don't want people to see me. It feels like everything about my body is exaggerated like some cartoon. It feels like those things shouldn't be there, like a deformity. Those thoughts make me want to itch. Wishing that if I were to pinch and scratch at it enough it would somehow erode away. I have a problem when it comes to picking, at least I am able to make sure no one else can see it. I pick at my skin and I tear up the inside of my cheeks. I won't say my body doesn't feel like it isn't mine, more like it's deformed and wrong. At the least, I can feel at peace when I am by myself. I know no one can see me when I am, and I don't have to think of my appearance. I distract myself, whether it be with school work or my artwork. My motivation is thinking that it won't be this way all my life. Even now I am saving up to start hormones and for top surgery. I am using my dysphoria and desires as a way to keep me going; to go to work and to learn how to cope with it. It's my ticket toward making myself look the way I know I should.

Danny

Additional Resources

Even though gender dysphoria is a very difficult thing to experience and deal with, there are very few resources online to help or find support.

 thetransbook.com/link/0201
thetransbook.com/link/0202

Dealing with feelings of dysphoria can be hard, and sometimes you need to reach out and talk to someone. The Trevor Project offers phone, text, and online chat support when you need it most. Trans Lifeline provides phone support that is run by trans people for trans and questioning people.

thetransbook.com/link/0203
This video by Phoenix Animations does a great job explaining what dysphoria is and feels like in under two minutes. It would be a great video to save and show to people when you have a hard time explaining dysphoria.

thetransbook.com/link/0204
This video by TeaTimeWithTBoys goes over the history of gatekeeping and how it's playing out in the present both in the trans and the medical communities.

CHAPTER 3

COMING OUT

You're probably asking yourself: "But how do I KNOW I'm transgender or gender-nonbinary?"

The good news is you're not the only one who's ever asked that question. The bad news is no one can answer that question but you. Even more frustrating, you will likely discover that the answer to that question changes over time.

In this chapter, we're going to explore how you can begin understanding your identity and how your identities can intersect and complement (or complicate) one another. We will also discuss the various "ways" to come out.

There's no one right way to do any of this, and it's okay to decide to not come out at all.

What Is Coming Out?

Coming out is most commonly described as the process of telling other people that your sexual orientation and/or gender identity is not straight and/or cisgender. More generally, coming out is the process of speaking your truth to the world. This is a really vulnerable process, though, because you're telling people how you understand your identity in hopes they will love, acknowledge, and accept you no matter what.

This probably sounds really overwhelming, but we come out about all kinds of things in our day to day lives. Sometimes it's coming out about low-stakes stuff: maybe you like a TV show that other people think is silly or nerdy, or maybe you get praised all the time for being good at math even if you don't like it. Other times, it's coming out about high-stakes stuff: maybe you have a chronic medical condition that other people have made judgments about in the past, or maybe you have a disability that other people don't usually notice.

Did you notice what all four examples above have in common? They are not easily seen from the outside. Who you know yourself to be inside doesn't have to match what you look like on the outside. Transgender and gender-nonbinary people will often delay coming out because they feel like they don't look "trans enough." There is no one right way to "be trans," though. If you are transgender or nonbinary, you're already doing it right just by being you.

What a person looks like and who they know themselves to be changes over time, and so will you. That's why coming out is an ongoing, lifelong process. You don't have to rush it.

Your Gender Timeline

A good way to start thinking about your gender identity is to think of it in the context of your past, present, and future.

Ask yourself:

1. How do I feel about the gender people assumed I was when I was born?
2. What gender do I wish people saw me as right now?
3. What gender do I want people to see me as when I'm an adult?

Take time to consider the similarities and differences between your answers. Do they tell you something you didn't know before? Did you get surprised by something? What might these answers tell you about where your journey might go next?

Knowing who you are is really hard to put into words. Especially when you're young and don't have the language or the experience to know who you are. I still don't know myself, but I can know one thing: "knowing" is really based on the language given to you. See, I always knew I was different from other kids, especially other girls. Did I know I was a boy? No, I didn't think that was an option for me, and the word trans had never even been uttered around me. It's all about  finding the word or words to describe yourself, or maybe you don't use any. Gender is interconnected with language. In reality, I always knew I was trans. But the language wasn't something I got until years later, when the gender roles were forced upon me. That's something I remember from my childhood, actually. I used to love wearing pink, and skirts, and dresses, and all of that, but the minute those became the things that categorize me as a "girl" and as "feminine," I rejected them. I haven't worn a dress or a skirt since I was maybe in seventh grade. It was this idea that as a "girl," I had to fulfill a certain expectation that just didn't fit right with me. I was the one going to play in the dirt; I was the kid who always wanted to play kickball even if I sucked; I was the kid always coming to school with scraped knees after playing in the street. Not to say girls can't do all of those things, but for me it felt as if there was a disconnect between what I felt inside and what people were seeing on the outside.

Coming Out to Yourself

Before you can come out to anyone else, you first have to come out to yourself. This can be a struggle for many people because we feel expected to act and behave in a particular way. Our parents, teachers, friends, and family put us into these gender boxes that don't fit who we know ourselves to be.

This dysphoria (which we explored in Chapter 2) is a conflict between how you feel inside and who everyone tells you you are on the outside. It can make you feel many different ways. You might be scared and confused. That doesn't mean you are wrong about your identity, it just means you are aware that the coming out process is going to require some work to integrate the part of you that you know into the part everyone else sees. You might feel strong and excited. You might feel anxious and excited. You

Developing Your Understanding of Your Own Identity

Take a few minutes to explore your understanding of gender and how that applies to your identity. There are no right or wrong answers, just as there is no right way to be a boy, a girl, or a nonbinary person!

- Describe what makes a boy a boy.
- Describe what makes a girl a girl.
- Describe what makes a person nonbinary.
- How do you know the difference between boys, girls, and nonbinary people?
- How would you know if someone wasn't a boy, a girl, or nonbinary?
- When does a person know they are a boy, a girl, or non-binary?
- When does a person know they aren't a boy, a girl, or nonbinary?
- Are you a boy? Are you a girl? Are you nonbinary? Are you something else? How do you know?
- If your body changed from female to male or male to female or binary to nonbinary, how would it change how you thought and felt about yourself?

might not be sure what you are feeling. However you feel, that is the right way for you to feel right now and you'll probably feel differently at different times over the coming days, weeks, months, and years.

Coming out to yourself is the most important step because it encourages you to dig deeper into your own understanding of gender in general, and of your gender identity in particular. This process is going to require you to develop your own personal understanding of gender and how that understanding applies to you.

These questions are designed to help you build a relationship with gender in general and how that applies to your own gender in particular. That process of thinking about gender will hopefully help it become easier to understand your own gender and, sometimes, to come out to yourself. Sometimes coming out to yourself happens slowly, other times it happens in a single moment. Either way, expect to feel many different emotions as you settle into the truth you are telling yourself. You might be sad, relieved, guilty, joyful, and all the things in between. Be gentle with yourself and take time to settle into your truth. Being confident in who you know yourself to be might even make coming out to others a little easier. And even if it doesn't, you'll know that you can trust yourself enough to be real with yourself.

Getting Ready to Come Out

We know we keep telling you this, but there's no one right way to come out. Everyone's coming out story is different— and not only from other people's coming out stories, their own coming out stories to different people will vary. You will come out many times. Each time you come out, you will have a new experience. And hopefully, after coming out a few times, you might even find that it gets a little easier.

One of the best things to do to set yourself up for success in coming out is to do some work ahead of time. This will act as a kind of defense as you go about your process of coming out to friends, family, teachers, and others.

Start by making a list of the benefits and risks of coming out. We've created a list below to get you started, but your list will likely include other pros and cons that apply to your particular experience.

While the benefits listed on the below list are pretty awesome, the risks are pretty scary. That's why it's important to spend some time creating a support network. A support network can be as large or small as you need, and is made up of people and resources you can reach out to quickly get help in an emergency. People in your support network might be a trusted teacher, a friend's parents, a local LGBTQIA+ center or church, or a support hotline you can reach out to, like the Trevor Project.

Benefits	**Risks**
• You can live openly and freely as yourself.	• People might not accept you or understand your identity.
• Your relationships (romantic, family, friends, etc.) will probably get stronger.	• You might lose some friendships or relationships.
• Your stress and anxiety will probably go down since you won't be spending a lot of energy on hiding.	• You might lose your job if you have one, or it might be hard to get a job.
• It will be easier to meet other transgender and gender-non-binary people.	• You might be kicked out of your house.
• You can feel more confident that people will like you for you.	• Your parents might stop supporting you financially.
• It can help set an example for others.	

It will also be helpful to collect resources for the people you are coming out to, so they'll have information available without having to hunt for it. You could provide them with links to online resources or prepare a "coming out packet" with printed materials. You can assemble your coming out packet using the resources you find at the end of each chapter of this book. Not only will providing these resources make it easier for them to get their questions answered, it will also allow you to present them with

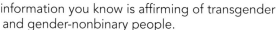

information you know is affirming of transgender and gender-nonbinary people.

The last step in getting ready is making a list of people you want to come out to, in the order you want to tell them. It's beneficial to tell the person who you think will take it the best and be really supportive of you first, so you can rely on them for help and support as you work your way down the list. You may be in a situation where you feel confident most people are going to be supportive and a simple numbered list will do. But if you're feeling a little less confident, try working through some of the questions below to see what they tell you.

Preparing to come out is important, but no amount of preparation is going to make your experience perfect. Take your time and be intentional about how you go through your process. At the end of the day, you are responsible only to yourself and making sure you are taken care of in this process. Other people's feelings and emotions about your coming out aren't about you. It's about their view of the world and their place in it. Do not let them make you feel guilty for speaking your truth. There are so many people in this world who are ready to support you for your truth.

Should I Come Out To _____?

- Why do I want to come out to this person?
- What do I want to say to them when I come out?
- Is now a good time to come out to them?
- What good things might they say to me after I come out to them?
- What are some bad things they might say to me after I come out to them?
- How can I deal with any bad things they say to me?
- Do I feel that I would be physically safe coming out to them?
- Do I feel like I can speak confidently to them and answer their questions?

Coming Out

So you've come out to yourself, you've prepared to come out to others, and now it's time to tell your first or second or third or hundredth person.

Each time you come out, think about what you want to tell the person and how you want to tell them. You can tell them in person, on video chat, by phone, writing them a letter, or just live your life and let them figure it out on their own.

When coming out to someone in person, be careful when choosing a time and place. If you're coming out to someone you are comfortable with, you may want to plan to have more time in a private space. This will allow the two of you to really connect with each other, and they'll have the opportunity to recognize and appreciate knowing more about you. For people who you may be less comfortable with, you might plan for a shorter meeting in a more public place. This way, if they react badly, it will be easier for you to move away from them, physically and emotionally, while they collect their own emotions and reactions. Your safety is most important, so do what you can to minimize the risk to yourself, even if that means not telling a particular person at all.

No matter how you think a person will react, always be prepared for a negative reaction. Some people need a longer amount of time to process and accept a coming out than others. But don't give up hope! Be patient and remember that the other person's reaction doesn't have any impact on who you are and how you exist in the world.

If you've already come out to people who took the news well, reach out to them to let them know you are coming out to someone new. Ask if they are willing to chat afterward, so you can debrief; or ask them to check in on you if they don't hear from you.

Coming Out to Parents

When preparing for and coming out to your parents, there are a few things you should do in addition to the steps talked about earlier in this chapter.

It's especially important to consider the benefits and risks of coming out to your parents. If they *are* supportive, they might be willing to help you get clothing that better expresses your gender, find a doctor and start HRT, or tell other family members. If they *aren't* supportive, it might lead to neglect, conversion therapy, or even being kicked out of the house. So, it's critical to have a support system in place ahead of time.

Coming out was probably one of the hardest experiences I've ever had to deal with. Coming out to my immediate family wasn't easy, and coming out to my extended family was even harder. The hardest person to come out to, however, was myself. When I was young and didn't know a lot about gender, I thought it was something that was set in stone for your whole life, something that only a select few had  the luxury to change. I don't know where I got this idea, but I always felt like being transgender was somehow off limits to me. Maybe I was just scared about what it would mean for my future, or maybe I felt as though transitioning would cause me to lose the life I already had. Because of this, I suppressed my feminine feelings because I thought it would make me different from everyone else, and, at the time, I really craved acceptance from the people around me. For many years, I would daydream about being a girl whenever I could, yet somehow I still couldn't connect the dots. I would imagine what it would be like if I had been born a girl, or if a wizard suddenly changed my gender one day. You would think that would be a pretty clear sign, but to me it was all a fairytale, a miracle I could never hope to experience. It wasn't until I was a senior in high school, when I had learned more about trans people and the lives they lived, that I realized I could be trans. At first I didn't know for sure, and, even if I did, I didn't want to face the judgement of those around me. I continued to think about it, though, and I realized that if I was the last person on earth and no one else's opinion mattered but mine, I would always choose to be a girl. Because of this, I knew that I would never be happy until I was true to myself in that regard, and that is how I found out who I really wanted to be.

Drace

If you decide to come out to your parents, consider the timing of the initial conversation (because it will likely be more than one). Holidays, for example, are not a good time. There is too much going on and too many claims on your parents' attention and time. Even if you just wait for a few days after the holiday, waiting will be well worth it.

Your parents may need more time than others to process your coming out. They've known you for a long time and have imagined what your future might look like. If your coming out wasn't part of the future they'd imagined for you, they might feel sad for a while. But at the end of the day, you are doing a kind and loving thing for them by letting them know exactly who their child is and how they will exist in the world.

Karen

Who should you come out to? People like me! That is, people who are talking and teaching about gender identity as a spectrum and that all gender identities are valid and beautiful. If this sounds like anyone you know, even if you don't know them very well, they are probably a great person to come out to first. They may also be able to offer you specific advice and support on coming out to others in your life.

Coming Out to Peers, Close Friends, and Romantic Partners

Just like with coming out to parents, you can follow the steps we've covered earlier in this chapter, along with some things you should consider as you come out to your peers, friends you've known for a long time, and your romantic partners.

Peers

Coming out to your peers—who are the people around your age that you go to school with, see at church, play sports with, or work with—is the hardest to plan for. You're not likely to come out

I don't know what the "right" label for me is, or if there even is one, but I'm out. I'm out as transgender, as using he/him pronouns, as "Tai." I don't know if that's "right," though. First I thought I was transgender, then bigender, then nonbinary, then genderfluid, and currently just plain questioning. First I thought I was straight, then gay, then androsexual, then pansexual, then asexual panromantic, then graysexual panromantic, all the while confused because I wanted to be some girls' boyfriend, some girls' girlfriend, and the same with various boys. Now I know I'm graysexual and somewhere on the aromantic spectrum, but where? I used to think I couldn't come out until I found the "right" label. I haven't found it yet (if it is out there, if there is such a thing), but I came out anyways. I did it because I felt like I couldn't live authentically otherwise, and being authentic is extremely important to me—I would rather lose friends and make enemies if it means I can be me—but that's not the case for everyone. Some people need their community, and others don't feel the need to advertise their LGBTQ+ identity, and others simply think it would distract from more important aspects, like their personality.

Tai

to each and every one of your peers one-on-one; they will most likely find out by word of mouth or through social media. This is complicated because you don't have any control over what other people say about you or what they post on social media. You'll need to be ready to have large groups of people find out and approach you with questions. Just remember: you don't owe anyone answers to their questions. *You* get to determine what specific information they find out and when.

Close Friends

Whether or not to come out to close friends will probably be one of the easier decisions to make. You likely have a good idea of how they'll feel and whether or not they're a safe person to confide in about your identity. Even if they're safe to come out to, they may not process the information as quickly as you'd like, just like family members who have known you for a long time. Thankfully, if they are supportive and ready to have your back, they can be a good support system as you come out to family, partners, and peers.

Romantic Partners

Coming out to romantic partners can be tricky. You likely have very strong feelings for each other, and if they are not expecting to hear that your gender identity is different than what they have come to know you as, it may be distressing or exciting. It all depends on the person. You deserve to have a partner who is respectful, supportive, and loving of you, and if your partner is not able to provide those things, it may mean your relationship has to end. At the end of the day, though, you owe your partner the truth about who you know yourself to be and you deserve to be happy.

Coming Out at School

School is a tricky place to navigate coming out. Your friends might be very supportive of you, but sometimes it's hard to tell how other students and teachers might react. It's important to have a good understanding of your school's overall climate for transgender and gender-nonbinary youth.

Ask these questions to determine how safe it might be to come out at your school:

- Is there a Gender and Sexuality Alliance (GSA) club or some other kind of student diversity group on campus?

- Are there gender neutral restrooms and locker rooms or rules about how transgender and gender-nonbinary students can use gendered restrooms and locker rooms?

- Are there anti-bullying rules that specifically protect students based on sexual orientation, gender identity, or gender expression?

- Are there supportive teachers, counselors, and other adults at school?

- Does my school have a religious philosophy that promotes a negative view of trans and nonbinary people? (Some religious schools do, while others are very inclusive and welcoming.)

- How would I feel about coming out at school?

- Would coming out at school make me unsafe? If so, what can I do to help make sure I stay safe?

If you feel like it would be a good idea and safe for you to come out at school, then follow the steps we talk about above. Make sure to have a plan, think about who you want to tell, and have a teacher or other adult ready to support and advocate for you on campus. You might identify a teacher who is an ally through word of mouth or if they have a safe space sticker or poster in their room. If your school doesn't allow teachers to post messages of support for LGBTQIA+ youth, then look for teachers who call out bullying, specifically bullying of LGBTQIA+ students.

Do What Is Right for You

Everyone's story is different and that applies to your coming out as well. For some people, coming out will be easy and joyful. For others, it will be one of the most difficult experiences of their lives.

We don't know how it will go for you. It's up to you to decide when, who, where, and how you want to come out. Your safety and happiness are important and finding the right mix of those might take some time and experimentation to figure out.

Kathryn

Something that is rarely talked about among transgender and gender-nonbinary people is the concept of de-transitioning. It's become a taboo topic because some people feel it proves the idea that being trans or nonbinary is a choice.

I came out as trans four times and de-transitioned (to various extents) four times before coming out a fifth time. For me, the fifth time was successful because I spent years coming to understand the power of the Trans Narrative (which we talk about in Chapter 6), and finally arrived at a point where I felt in control of my transition. Before, I was trying so desperately to become a woman, but the reality was that I always had been a woman.

In my case, de-transition was a way to regain control of my life, but there are many reasons a person might de-transition. They may do it for safety reasons, or family reasons, or medical reasons, or any other reason. All of these reasons are valid and do not invalidate the reality of trans and nonbinary people's identities.

Additional Resources

thetransbook.com/link/0301
The Trevor Project's "Coming Out as You" guide is a great resource for anyone coming out as LGBTQIA+ and their friends.

thetransbook.com/link/0302
CenterLink's website allows you to search for LGBTQIA+ centers near you. These are great places to access in-person support and community.

thetransbook.com/link/0303
We searched YouTube for some good coming out videos but there are too many to list, so just hop on and do your own search to learn how others handled their coming out.

thetransbook.com/link/0304
PFLAG is an organization comprised of many grassroots chapters across the United States that support the parents, friends, and allies of LGBTQIA+ people. Many chapters also offer opportunities for LGBTQIA+ people to meet and receive support from one another.

BODY

CHAPTER 4

DEVELOPING BODIES

The physical, biological, and sexual changes a body goes through from birth until death are usually focused on the toddler years and on the teenage years. During these times, there is more change in the physical body than at any other time during life. This chapter focuses on the teenage years. The changes that happen during the teenage years are generally referred to as puberty. People who are trans may experience puberty in similar or in very different ways from people who are cis.

Regardless of gender identity, puberty is one of those pieces of life that everyone has stories about. It can be a rite of passage. It can be horrible or great or anything in between. It can be a time to learn new things about ourselves and the people around us. It can feel like you're becoming more yourself or less yourself. The personal stories that come from puberty become some of the things we tell new people when we are getting to know them: When did you first... How did you feel when... Who did you tell?

Talking or reading about puberty (or any of the highly gendered aspects of the human body) can be particularly hard if your body doesn't align with your identity. We use biologically related terminology in this chapter, like the names of hormones, genitals, etc. Be gentle with yourself as you make your way through this content. The days when your dysphoria is particularly high are bad days to try and make your way through this content. If it feels like you will never be able to read this chapter, ask a friend to *go through and cross out all of the gendered words and write in words that feel more right to you.*

Just as your body is yours, this book is yours, too. Change it to make it fit you!

Types of Changes

The types of changes that occur during puberty are not different for transgender, gender-fluid, and gender-nonbinary people. A person's gender identity does not, on its own, impact the physical process of puberty or any other biological processes, unless the person is changing this process through medical interventions.

Without interventions, most bodies begin to go through puberty somewhere between the ages of 9 and 12. The process usually ends between ages 16 and 20. That means, unless you are on hormone blockers, your body has probably begun the process and may or may not have finished it.

Puberty means changes in the following body systems:

- **Hormones.** Every person has some combination of androgens (which includes testosterone and are usually thought of as male hormones) and estrogens (which are usually thought of as female hormones). The release of these hormones into the body marks the beginning of puberty and begins the rest of the physical changes.

- **Secondary sexual characteristics.** Most of the physical changes that people notice are in this category. These changes continue throughout puberty and happen on their own unique time schedule. When these changes happen, and they are different from what your gender identity says they should be, it can be hard to manage your feelings and your relationship with your body.

- **Primary sexual characteristics.** These changes are ones that allow your body to reproduce. These include things like ovulating, menstruating, and sperm production. (The specifics about each of these processes are in the next chapter on reproduction.)

However, while there is a wide range of physical changes, the way puberty is medically assessed is through five stages described by changes to the breasts, penis, and pubic hair, called the Tanner Stages.

More About Hormones

It usually takes a little while for a person's body to begin to change, and so most people don't even realize when the hormones that start puberty begin to be released. These hormones are released by the ovaries and the testicles in response to signals from the brain. All people, regardless of sex assigned at birth or gender identity, have both androgens and estrogens in their bodies. The balance of these hormones is what influences the development of secondary and primary sexual characteristics (puberty).

There are medications called hormone blockers that stop hormone production related to puberty. They prevent puberty from happening until a young person understands their gender identity on a deeper level and is ready to either stop using hormone blockers or to begin hormone replacement therapy. Blockers cannot be continued indefinitely because of the potential impact on bone health. Clinics around the world prescribe hormone blockers differently, but usually only in Tanner Stages 2 and 3. How long you might be on hormone blockers will depend on your particular situation.

When the hormones in a person's body are making changes that are not in alignment with their gender identity, it can be scary and overwhelming. Hormone replacement therapy (HRT) shifts that process. HRT can begin at the same time as blockers, when blockers are stopped, or at any point after puberty begins. HRT shifts the changes associated with puberty so the body develops in a way that matches the person's gender identity.

More About Secondary Sexual Characteristics

Secondary sexual characteristics are physical changes that develop during puberty that distinguish "women" from "men" like average height, voice tone, facial hair, fat distribution, etc., and are not related to reproduction. There are some changes that everyone goes through, like growing pubic hair and the body sweating and smelling more and differently. All of the body changes you can see, hear, or smell on another person when they have all their clothes on, along with a few others like pubic hair, are secondary sexual characteristics. After hormones begin to be released at the beginning of puberty, secondary sexual characteristics are the first changes.

Secondary sexual characteristics are highly influenced by androgens and estrogens. When hormone blockers are started early in the puberty process, secondary sexual characteristics are easily repressed. With the introduction of hormones that are in alignment with a person's gender identity, secondary sexual characteristics grow and develop in ways that are supportive of the person's identity and experiences of dysphoria are fewer and farther between. (See Chapter 2 for more information on dysphoria.)

If a person goes through full puberty development, their secondary sexual characteristics are much more difficult to change and require surgery to bring them into alignment with the person's gender identity. Preventing those long-term difficulties is why so many people are excited about the possibility of either hormone blockers or getting HRT. It is not always possible to do either of those medical treatments, due to money, insurance, access, or other problems. But if you are not able to get on either blockers or hormones, that doesn't mean you are stuck. There are so many ways, big and small, for you to take steps to live your truth. This gets easier as you get older and have more control over your life, of course, but it's not something you are totally without, even now. For more ideas and thoughts on living as yourself, see Chapter 7.

Karen

Bodies change—and then they keep on changing. There will never be a point in your life at which your body is "done." For some people, this is a bummer, because they fall in love with their body at a certain point in time. For other people, this is a good thing because it means that even if you don't like your body at a certain moment, it's going to keep changing, and you have control over some of that process.

Puberty sucks. The constant fluctuations in hormones, the weird changes in your body, the awkwardness that I sincerely hope is temporary - it's all uncomfortable, and the narrative surrounding puberty doesn't make it any better. Nearly every conversation I've ever had about my puberty experience has resulted in at least one person saying: "It's just part of your journey into womanhood." Great. That makes me feel so much better. I have no desire to be a woman. I don't care about growing breasts, I don't care about being able to carry a child, I don't care about ninety percent of the things associated with "womanhood," yet that's all anyone seems to be talking about.

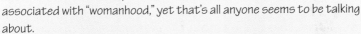

I think members of the trans+ community often have enormous difficulty with our developing bodies because they remind us of the identities we are trying so desperately to leave behind. I hate getting my period because it's a monthly reminder that I have a female body. I hate my breasts because they get in the way of my looking good in suits. I hate my curves because they make it damn near impossible for me to wear masculine clothing.

Though I find nearly everything about puberty to be intolerable, I do like that it is associated with growth and change. Yes, people say these years are about becoming a woman but, really, these years are about becoming me. I claim my adolescence as my own; I am figuring out who I am. Though my body is developing into something I am not, I am developing into something closer to what I am.

E.

Primary sexual characteristics are the parts of the body that are directly related to reproduction. The majority of these are present at birth but go through changes and growth during puberty. These changes usually happen in the middle part of puberty, and they also make it hard to manage your emotions if they are not in alignment with your gender identity.

The two most common primary sexual characteristics are closely tied to gamete development (that is, the development of sperm and eggs, which are the cells that can result in reproduction) and pregnancy:

- Vagina, uterus, and ovaries
- Penis and tesicles

The ovaries begin to produce mature eggs as a result of pubertal hormones. Approximately once a month, one of the ovaries will release an egg into the fallopian tubes. This is called ovulation. Ovulation will continue, unless otherwise stopped, until menopause in older adulthood. If there is sperm present in the fallopian tube at the time of ovulation, it may enter a released egg. At that point, it will make its way down the fallopian tube and embed in the uterus, resulting in a pregnancy. More frequently, however, the egg makes its way down the fallopian tube unfertil-

Kathryn

It's really important to understand that everyone has a mix of estrogen and testosterone in their bodies. When I first started medical transition, I couldn't wait to get rid of all my testosterone and replace it with estrogen. So I was really surprised to find out that I still needed some testosterone in my body, and it gave me some pretty severe dysphoria. At that point in my transition, I definitely wanted to make a binary change, and having to keep some testosterone in me seemed to go against that. The older I get though, and the longer I'm in transition, the more and more I like that I have both kinds of hormones. It doesn't invalidate my identity to have testosterone, and it makes me feel more secure in the parts of me that feel more nonbinary.

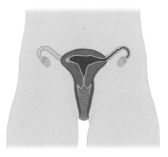

ized. When it does not embed in the lining of the uterus, the lining pulls away from the uterine wall and slowly flows out of the body through the vagina. This is called the menses, or period.

The testicles begin to produce sperm as a result of pubertal hormones. Beginning at the point when the testicles start to work, the person will, unless otherwise stopped, continue to create and develop sperm for the rest of their life. When the person is sexually aroused, mature sperm will be pushed from the testicles up through the vas deferens to the base of the penis. There it will mix with fluid from the seminal vesicles and the prostate. The sperm plus the additional fluid is called semen.

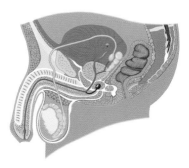

The most noticeable primary sexual changes during puberty are the beginning of the menses, or period, and the enlargement of the penis. The existence of the organs that are part of these changes are not changeable in any way other than surgery. The shifts that take place during puberty, however, are somewhat brought back to pre-pubescent levels through hormones and can be fully reversed through surgery.

I started puberty the first time around in the beginning of middle school. Ever since then, I knew something seemed a bit off. I didn't really know that there was a biological difference between genders until I learned about puberty. There's really not a lot to say about female puberty other than breasts growing, a bit of acne, and a period every month. My process of hitting female puberty basically went by the book according to the videos they show us in elementary school...other than me being uncomfortable in my body. I just thought everyone felt the same as I did.

During female puberty, I learned about what being transgender meant and, suddenly, everything made so much more sense. I learned about hormones, surgery, and gender affirming actions I could take to feel more comfortable in my body. Shortly after, I began to pursue hormone replacement therapy when I was 13 or 14 years old. After a long while of back and forth between counselors, doctors, parents, and psychiatrists, I was finally able to take my first testosterone shot on July 31, 2017 at the age of 15 years old.

Hitting puberty for the second time was so much different and more difficult than the first time. When starting hormones for your second puberty, the doctor tells you what to expect, but you'll never be prepared enough. The first thing I noticed was my hunger. I was always hungry and moody. After a few months, things simmer down and more physical changes begin to happen rather than emotional. Emotionally, you just begin to feel more at home within yourself.

Johnny

Puberty was a confusing period in my life and a time where I would fight both myself and my parents. As my body began to curve and develop, I seemed to care less and less about my appearance. I've come to realize now that I was just so insecure about my body and myself that I became overwhelmed and couldn't find the motivation to fix my appearance. All I would wear in middle school were T-shirts, sweatpants, and hoodies. I would also leave my hair a complete mess. I was  noticing other girls all the time, and so, at first, I thought I was just a lesbian. A very butch lesbian. Now, I did try the dresses and makeup. For a while, I even forced myself to wear them more often, thinking that my tomboyishness was a phase. Although, as I began to research my feelings, I found the term transgender and it all clicked. I stayed with that thought for a while before deciding to come out a second time. As expected, my parents didn't let me transition at first. A couple months after coming out, I couldn't quite take having to lie to myself anymore. And so I grabbed some scissors. I took a deep breath and stood with a lock of hair between the blades forever before finally bringing them together. After the first lock of hair, there was no turning back. Before that, I had never seen my mother more angry at me. I realized that if I did not move forward in my transition, neither would my parents. So I began to push, and haven't stopped since.

Access

The World Professional Association for Transgender Health (WPATH) currently recommends that parents, teenagers, and children give informed consent for fully reversible medication interventions (hormone blockers) and that they live for a year as their gender identity before beginning any partially reversible or irreversible medical interventions (HRT, surgery, etc.). This kind of gatekeeping is something that adults, including doctors and parents, want, while teenagers want informed consent to be sufficient to begin HRT. It is possible WPATH will shift their recommendations to informed consent for partially reversible interventions in the future. In fact, we hope they have already done that by the time you're reading this book. (For a lot more information on these issues, see Chapter 8.)

Being frustrated, hurt, angry, and many more emotions at not being able to access medical treatment that would help you feel better in your body is shitty and exhausting. It's not your fault the medical establishment is still trying to control your body. They try to control a lot of people's bodies without much cause or reason. Part of what we're hoping to do with this book is to give you back some control.

What's In a Name?

Trans guys have all kinds of names for their periods! From Shark Week to MANstruation, these terms help trans guys handle something their bodies are doing that might cause a lot of physical discomfort and dysphoria.

In Your Body

No one can tell you what puberty will feel like for you. There are so many different ways that people can feel about it, although there are few positive feelings for trans youth who are not yet taking HRT. When you are able to experience puberty in a way that is bringing you closer to looking like your gender identity, it can be a fun and exciting experience.

The following pages detail the different kinds of medical treatments available to make your body change in ways to bring it closer to your gender identity.

Fully Reversible Interventions

The most common fully reversible intervention is hormonal birth control. This serves to stop the period, which is often the cause of the most intense gender dysphoria for trans boys. The other common option, as already mentioned, are hormone blockers.

Hormonal birth control works for trans boys to stop their periods and generally reduce the amount of estrogens in their body. They have been well researched, used for decades, and are generally considered to be safe and effective.

Using hormone blockers to put off puberty for trans teens is a relatively new practice, however, and so research is not complete. Most research says hormone blockers are safe. In fact, they make it easier for trans and gender-nonconforming youth to feel more emotionally and psychologically stable during puberty. One potential negative side effect of hormone blockers is for people with penile tissue who might later want genital surgery to build a vagina. Taking blockers might prevent the penis from growing enough to later build a vagina. There are, however, other options like using a skin graft or colon tissue for this purpose.

Partially Reversible Interventions

Hormone therapy to masculinize or feminize a person's secondary sexual characteristics are partially reversible ways to influence the gender of bodies. The hormone treatments teenagers use for HRT are different from the treatments adults use, which is why it's important to see a pediatric endocrinologist who specializes in prescribing HRT for teenagers. See Chapter 8 for more information about the details of HRT.

Irreversible Interventions

Medical interventions that cannot be reversed are surgical. Whether and what kind of surgeries a person wants to get depends on many things. A person is no more or less trans because they have or have not had surgeries.

Chest surgery involves removal of excess chest tissue or an increase of chest tissue. These surgeries are relatively well understood and have been effectively carried out for many years.

Genital surgeries are more complex and there is a shorter history of effectiveness. Other kinds of surgeries, including body contouring, facial feminization or masculinization, and more, are also possible. Details of these surgeries are all included in Chapter 8.

Should I Do It?

We can't answer that question for you. All we can do, really, is tell you how other people have felt and encourage you to talk with your family (if they are safe and supportive) and your treatment team.

Not all trans people want to change their bodies. Some trans people feel comfortable in their body, even with all of the puberty changes that came with it without medical intervention. Their gender identity is wide and inclusive enough to live in the body they have.

Not all trans people can change their bodies. There are many barriers, especially for people under 18, who want to feminize or masculinize their bodies. From uncooperative parents and medical staff to financial and insurance barriers, access to blockers, hormone therapy, and surgery can feel like it will never happen. There are small steps you can take right now (see Chapter 6) until you're old enough to make your own decisions about your body.

Some trans people want to and are able to change their bodies. The overwhelming majority of teenagers who feel gender dysphoria and who take steps to change their bodies to be more in alignment with who they are never look back. They feel better emotionally, physically, and psychologically. They're able to connect with their friends and families better. They are able to focus on and reach their academic and personal goals.

For most people, there are no perfect solutions. We hope you are able to find the solution that works best for you!

Puberty is a strange time in everyone's life, but for me it felt exceptionally strange. My body began to change quickly, and shifting hormone levels began affecting my behavior. While some of the changes I didn't mind, others made me uncomfortable in a way I couldn't describe. Even though I started feeling like a stranger in my own body, I still had pride in who I was becoming, because I knew I was closer  to meeting the expectations of the adults in my life. They wanted me to grow up to be a tall, strong, confident man, and that's what I was on track to becoming. Even though I was enjoying my body less and less, I was enjoying the acceptance much more. What I wasn't enjoying, though, was my changing behavior. As a kid going through puberty, I felt more confident than ever due to the acceptance from others and my increased testosterone, and it really showed. I was louder and wilder than ever and, even though it was fun at the moment, I look back and really regret the way I acted. It was like a high I couldn't come down from, and it caused me to be competitive, loud, and aggressive to the people I really cared about. It wasn't until puberty began to fade, and my behavior returned to normal, that I realized the damage I had done. I fell into a great depression after that, and from that day forth I hated who I had become. It felt like puberty had taken everything away from me, and left me in a body I no longer cared about. It took me years to move on, and even longer to realize why the whole experience hurt so much, because I was being doomed to a fate I didn't want, to grow up and grow old as a man. I am truly lucky that didn't end up being the case.

Drace

Additional Resources

The majority of information about puberty out there in the world is about cis puberty. While sometimes there is a sentence or two about trans youth experiencing puberty a little bit differently, there is not a lot that has been created about a trans-specific experience of puberty, but these resources all provide some information.

thetransbook.com/link/0401
TRANSYOUTH Documentary

thetransbook.com/link/0402
Puberty Information for Teens By the Palo Alto Medical Foundation

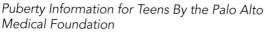

thetransbook.com/link/0403
Challenges for Transgender Children During Puberty (and other videos!)

thetransbook.com/link/0404
The Body Is Not An Apology
by Sonya Renee Taylor
When it comes to understand your body and the changes that are a part of it, one of the best resources out there is this book—and anything else by Taylor!

CHAPTER 5

REPRODUCTION AND HAVING CHILDREN

Take your time with this chapter and shift the language if you need to, taking care of yourself first. The introduction to this section has specific ideas on how to do that.

Raising children is something that some people feel very passionately about while others feel neutral or negatively about it. Regardless of whether you hope to parent someday or not: You can indeed get pregnant—or get someone else pregnant—even if you, they, or both of you are on hormone blockers or on hormone replacement therapy.

So even if parenting is not something you want as a part of your life—that's totally fine!—you should still read this chapter because it includes information that may become important for you in your own life or when you support friends in their lives.

If parenting is something you do want as part of your life, it is definitely something trans people regularly do. There just aren't very many stories or examples of trans parents out in the world, particularly trans parents who began their parenting journey after they were out—at least not yet.

All About Reproduction

Reproduction

Reproduction requires two different kinds of gametes. These are the kinds of cells that merge together to create the possibility of human life. Human gametes are called eggs and sperm. People with eggs usually also have ovaries, fallopian tubes, a uterus, and a vagina. People with sperm usually also have testicles, vas deferens, and a penis. Some people have eggs, some people have sperm, and some people have neither. No one has both. Below are descriptions of the ways gametes are formed, merge, and develop into a pregnancy. (Go back to Chapter 4 for pictures of the anatomy described in this chapter.)

Eggs develop and are then released from an ovary into a fallopian tube in a process called ovulation. Ovulation happens about once a month and the two ovaries in the body usually take turns creating each month's egg.

Sperm are created in the testicles and mature in the epididymis. During sexual arousal when the penis is erect, the sperm make their way through the vas deferens to the base of the penis where they mix with other fluids to become ejaculate called semen. From here, the semen is pushed down the urethra and out of the head of the penis when an orgasm and ejaculation occur.

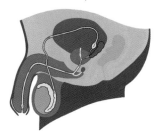
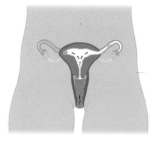

Sperm are most likely to meet an egg when they have been ejaculated into a vagina. From the vagina, sperm make their way up through the cervix and uterus and into the fallopian tubes. If there are sperm present when ovulation occurs (or within a few hours after that), one of the sperm may make its way into the egg. This process is called fertilization and creates a zygote. This is the very first step of a pregnancy.

Usually there are no sperm in the fallopian tubes before or during ovulation, so the egg continues down into the uterus where it dissolves. When this happens, the lining of the uterus pulls away and leaves the body through the vagina. This is called menstruation, having your period, a visit from Aunt Flow, or a variety of other terms.

People of all genders can either get pregnant or get someone else pregnant depending on their gamete situation. If you want to biologically reproduce, you probably can. If you do not want to biologically reproduce, there are steps you can take to prevent that from happening, in both immediate and long-term sexual connections.

Getting Pregnant

There are several important things for people who are trans, and who want to biologically conceive, to know:

1. Testosterone can stop the period, however, gametes may still be produced by the ovaries, which means pregnancy is possible.

2. Estrogen can stop or otherwise interfere with gamete production, however, it does not necessarily completely eliminate it.

3. Top surgery does not change whether a person is able to reproduce. Bottom surgery may or may not change whether a person is able to reproduce, depending on the specifics of their surgical process.

4. Many doctors recommend, if someone is going on hormones and they think they may want to biologically conceive later in life, that they store and freeze their gametes for potential future use.

Other than these notes, the biological reproduction process is basically the same for people who are trans as it is for everyone else.

One of the few undebatable truths of humanity is that babies are cute. With their puffy cheeks, shining eyes, and tiny fingers, it's not hard to understand why baby fever is so very contagious.

Regardless, I don't think I want to have children. I have so much admiration for people who choose to bear children, and for those who can find joy in that experience, but I don't think that will ever be me. Carrying a child is a life experience that is entirely associated with femininity, and at this moment in time, I cannot imagine myself being comfortable enough in my identity, in my body, and in my presentation to embrace womanhood in that way. If I am pregnant, everyone will see me as a woman, and I'm not comfortable with that.

Honestly, though, all of that could change. I'm sixteen years old, and I still have a lot to figure out. My decision about having children depends on the path my life takes from this point forward. It depends on my career, it depends on my partner, it depends on my financial stability, it depends on my mental health, it depends on my physical health, it depends on a lot of things that I can't predict at the moment, and that's okay.

The decision of whether or not to have children is incredibly personal, and I don't want to make it right now, nor do I have to. The one thing I know right now is that I have no desire to carry a child myself. But it's impossible to know what the future holds, so I will just trust that I'll be able to make the best decision for myself later.

E.

When semen, which includes sperm, is ejaculated into the vagina before or around the time of ovulation, there is a chance of pregnancy. Here are a few pieces of information that are important in understanding when someone can get pregnant:

1. Ovulation typically takes place 12-16 days after the first day of a person's period.

2. Ovulation could take place either earlier or later in the cycle because a person's rhythms are different, because of hormone fluctuation, or even because of stress. Some people even ovulate differently when they travel across time zones!

3. An average period can last between three and ten days.

4. Sperm can live in the fallopian tubes for up to seven days.

When put together, this means that if someone had a period for seven days (a pretty normal length), and then ovulated on day 13, they definitely could have gotten pregnant from condomless sex they had when they were still on their period.

There are, of course, other ways to get pregnant than through penile-vaginal intercourse. When two people who only have one type of gamete between them want to have a child, they often pick one of the below methods. They all require donation of the other kind of gamete, either eggs or sperm.

Semen can be ejaculated and then taken to the person with the ovaries who wants to get pregnant. The semen can either be kept at body temperature for 20 minutes or less or it can be frozen and thawed through a medical procedure. It is then put into the vagina or the uterus, depending on the specific medical protocol.

Sperm can also be extracted from semen and put with an egg in a laboratory setting. The resulting embryos are either frozen or put into the uterus immediately. Standard protocol is to transfer either one or two embryos to the uterus, where they will hopefully embed in the uterus and develop into a pregnancy.

Couples who want to conceive, and who include someone who has a uterus and wants to carry a pregnancy to term and give birth, are able to accept a donation of semen and move forward fairly easily through the pregnancy and birth process.

Couples with either only sperm or no gametes at all typically face a more difficult, or at least more expensive, path to biological reproduction because finding someone to carry the pregnancy to term and then give birth requires substantially more effort than finding someone to ejaculate into a cup. The medical process, however, is exactly the same.

When Pregnancy Won't Happen

Because there is often confusion about what can cause pregnancy, here's a list of sexual acts entirely incapable of resulting in a pregnancy (more details on each of these acts in Chapter 13):

- Kissing
- Over and under the clothes touching
- Mutual masturbation
- Oral sex
- Anal sex

And pregnancy will almost never, although in theory could, happen as a result of these sexual acts:

- Ejaculation with semen on a vulva (rather than in a vagina)
- Ejaculation on a sex toy, which is then inserted into a vagina

Preventing Pregnancy

Because there are so few ways for pregnancy to actually occur, preventing it should be easy. But for couples who have two different kinds of gametes and who want to engage in penis-in-vagina intercourse, it's easier said than done! Most couples with different kinds of gametes who are having penis-in-vagina intercourse will begin a pregnancy within a year without preventive measures. What's important to know is there are many ways to prevent pregnancy should you be interested in the kind of sex that brings together the two kinds of gametes. For a full introduction to this topic, see Chapter 14.

Pregnancy and Birth

After the two gametes come together to form one cell, it starts to divide and moves down the fallopian tube into the uterus. Then it implants in the lining of the uterus and begins to develop. The forty weeks of pregnancy (which start on the first day of the last period) are divided up into three trimesters.

Since I was small, I knew I didn't want to have biological children. At the time, I justified it with the logic that there's already overpopulation, there are too many children who never get adopted into the loving families they deserve, plus morning sickness and childbirth are no fun. Now, I wonder if it wasn't just the idea of being pregnant giving me dysphoria, or the idea of having sex as someone

who doesn't experience that kind of attraction. It's also a factor in terms of medical transitioning. Hormone replacement therapy can cause people to be sterile, and while I don't expect to have biological children, it's still a big decision. Most LGBTQ+ people don't have LGBTQ+ parents, so there's also this drive we have to raise our kids in a more accepting, tolerant environment that lends itself to authentic self-exploration. Whenever I think of raising kids, I think of gender neutral names, of not introducing the concept of gender to my children as they grow up, to seeing them as people first. But I can't protect them—they will see the binary enforced every time they leave their home, they will see how society treats their parent(s), and they may decide I'm in the wrong, that they want to be nothing like me. They may resent me for confusing them. Like anyone else, I want to raise my children to share my beliefs and values of authenticity and tolerance, and, like anyone else, I think I'm right to do so, but who's to know?

Tai

The first trimester, which lasts from about week 1 to week 12, is when the majority of the basic elements of a human body begin. This includes the nervous and cardiovascular systems, among others, which will eventually develop into some of the most important parts of the fetus. The rate of miscarriage, or when a pregnancy ends because it is not viable, is highest during the first trimester. This is also the time when the pregnant person can have the biggest negative impact by ingesting foods, alcohol, and/or drugs that harm fetal development. The pregnant person may feel sick, tired, and generally physically worn out during this trimester.

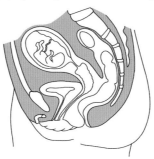

The second trimester is when the fetal organs do the majority of developing to their viable forms. By the end of the second trimester (week 26), many fetuses are able to live with medical support if they are born at that time. The pregnant person is likely to feel the most energetic and like themselves during this trimester.

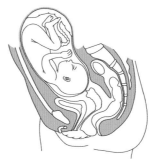

The third trimester is when fetuses grow, gain weight, and finish developing the lungs, eyes, hair, and a few more systems. Thirty-seven weeks after the first day of the last period is when the fetus is considered to be "term" and would not be considered too early if they were born. Forty weeks is the average length of a pregnancy and after 42 weeks, the fetus would be considered "late." In the third trimester, the pregnant person is likely to feel tired from carrying around a baby all the time.

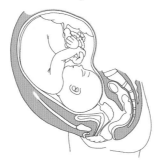

The birth process can either be a vaginal birth or a cesarean section, which is a surgical birth. Vaginal births are usually safer for both the birthing person and the baby. When there is a problem, like if the opening of the vagina is covered by the placenta or the baby is situated across the uterus rather than head or butt down, a surgical birth is necessary.

Some people feel very passionately about giving birth, while others do not. How you personally feel about being pregnant and giving birth (or definitely not doing those things!) does not have to be related to your gender identity. There are men who wish they could give birth and women who never want anything to do with it. Whether you want to take part in this process is something that is uniquely up to you and no one else. Listen to yourself about what feels right, rather than cultural stereotypes about what people of any gender are supposed to do or not supposed to do.

All About Parenting

Ways to Become a Parent

Biological reproduction—through a penis ejaculating into a vagina or a lab process—is only one approach to becoming a parent. Here are a few examples of ways people become parents:

- International adoption (connecting with a child in an orphanage in another country, traveling to that country with the support of the orphanage, gaining legal custody of the child, and bringing them home)

- Domestic adoption (connecting with a child in state custody or with a woman who is pregnant and wants to find adoptive parents for the baby and going through the associated legal processes to bring the child or baby home)

- Foster parenting (connecting with a child in state custody who you care for on an ongoing basis)

- Partnering or marrying someone who has a child and stepping into a parent role with that child

- Connecting with an emerging or existing family to become part of their chosen family and stepping into a parent role with the children

- Stepping into a service-based organization that provides support for young people including schools, churches, nonprofits, community centers, and more, and engaging with the babies, children, and youth as parents.

As you can see, the options for becoming a parent are wide ranging. What's most important about being a parent is that you stand as a support for the young people in both practical (providing housing, food, transportation, education, etc.) and impractical (love, fun, humor, stuff animals, etc.) details.

What Does It Mean to Be a Trans Parent?

Have you seen the show *Transparent*? It took the world by storm as one of the most public representations of a trans person coming out and living their truth. It ran for five seasons, ending in 2018. It shows one example of how someone who is trans can parent. But this is far from the only option. One of the most striking ways *Transparent* is different from how many of you reading this book might experience being a parent is that the main character, Maura, came out as an adult, after her children were also adults. Rather than growing up thinking of their mother as their mother, they thought of her as their father. For you, reader, your children can be born into your family and grow up knowing you as yourself.

But the reality is that there are as many ways to parent as there are people. Every person will find their own path, regardless of whether they lean toward a masculine, feminine, or androgynous approach. Each and every parent brings special aspects to their

One of the biggest regrets I will ever have in my life is not being able to experience carrying a child myself. It's a fact I've tried again and again to come to terms with, yet I can never shake from my mind how unfair it is that I never will. Ever since I knew what pregnancy was, I felt like I deserved to experience it, but the genetic lottery was not kind to me in that sense. I used to always tell myself I didn't want to have kids, but I still felt like I was missing out on what would have been a really important part of my life. I've always loved the feeling of helping and caring for others, and it only feels right to be able to nurture a new spirit coming into this world. I know I can always do this by adopting or fostering children (and I am definitely considering doing so), but I feel like some part of me still feels empty knowing pregnancy will never be an option for me. In terms of raising children, I'm at least glad that I can now be a mother to my kids rather than a father. Growing up, the idea of being a dad was really scary to me, and I could never see myself raising a child (mostly because I could never imagine myself as a masculine adult). Now that I have transitioned, and I feel more at home in my body and how I am perceived by those around me, I feel much more comfortable with the idea of raising kids. Regardless of my feelings toward pregnancy, I hope that if I ever choose to raise kids in this life I am at least a good mother to them, and I hope they always feel loved.

Drace

parenting. Maybe they pass on a love of books or running or a killer sense of style. Maybe they teach their little ones to dance or play the piano or light a fire. Kissing hurt knees, cuddling good night, and eating breakfast together are all gender-free activities that all parents can bring to their little ones.

One of the most important things a parent can offer their children is a strong role model and example of living their truth authentically, honestly, and compassionately. Being out and trans is one amazing way to provide that lifelong guidance to young people.

Children Are Great! And They're Only One Part of Life.

So if you aren't interested in parenting, don't sweat it. Maybe you'll change your mind later—and maybe you won't. What's most important is that you're making your own decisions about whether and when you become a parent.

Karen

I always knew I wanted children—and now I'm lucky enough to parent three of them. It is a lot of work. I never wish that someone who doesn't want to parent accidentally ends up parenting. This should be a choice that comes from something inside you, not something you're guilted into or feel obligated to do. There are plenty of humans on our small planet—only add to that if you feel deeply compelled. And, happily, there are plenty of ways to parent without getting pregnant or getting your partner pregnant! You can be every bit of a parent to a child who you don't have any biological connection to. I know this for certain because I don't have a biological connection to one of my three children.

Additional Resources

There are not a lot of resources about trans people parenting. Hopefully in the coming years there will be more and more!

 thetransbook.com/link/0501
A Family in Transition: Two fathers and the baby girl they never expected.

thetransbook.com/link/0502
Transgender Parents: A film by Remy Huberdeau

thetransbook.com/link/0503
Lamda Legal: FAQ About Transgender Parenting.

I am a transgender male and should be able to reproduce. Having children is definitely something I'd like to do one day, but I wouldn't want to be the one to carry the child. There are many ways transgender people could arrange having children. You could ask your doctors for surrogates, artificial insemination, in vitro, or freezing your eggs or sperm. I'd personally go the route of finding a surrogate to carry my child for me or if I marry a cisgender woman then I would let her carry the child by artificial insemination or in vitro fertilization. I've seen cases where transgender men and cis women are able to have children together. If I were to marry a cis male, then I'd definitely go the surrogate path. I would find a close friend or family member who would be willing to carry my child for me and have enough trust to be responsible for my future baby for nine months. I don't really see myself not having a kid.

Johnny

I have dreams of having a family someday, like every person does. Although being a trans man, I do not want to have a baby of my own. At the time of writing this, I am still pre-everything, and I know for a fact I want to finish my transition as quickly as possible. I wouldn't want to keep my breasts to breastfeed, and having a baby would bring me so much more dysphoria from what I am experiencing now. Even so, I know that I want a child in my life. Somebody I can guide and unconditionally love. What I want to do later in life is to foster children and adopt a child. I don't see the point in creating a new life if there are so many lives that still need saving. Currently, as a teacher, I have seen how intelligent, talented, and kind children can be. I've also seen how that potential is destroyed by parents who may be going through painful processes in their lives or if they just simply are not good parents. Although it is impossible to help every child, I always strive to make sure they are in a happier and safer environment when they are around me. That's something I don't want to stop doing, so I want to take in the children who may have not been wanted in the first place.

Danny

TRANSITIONING

CHAPTER 6

DISMANTLING THE TRANS NARRATIVE

There are so many pressures facing transgender and gender-nonbinary people, especially the spoken and unspoken expectations of society about what steps they should take in their transitions and how fast they should go. These expectations about what trans people's stories should be like is what we call the "Trans Narrative," and it prevents exploration, experimentation, and self-acceptance.

In this chapter, we'll explore the history of the Trans Narrative, especially as it has played out in the United States, and talk about ways you can break out of the narrative and write your own amazing story.

The Power of Stories

Humans love stories. We love to have them told to us, we love to tell them to others, we love to create our own stories, and we love to apply those stories to the world around us. Stories are very powerful because they help shape the way we think about the people and places and events that we encounter every day.

If you've learned about storytelling in school, you're probably pretty familiar with the basic structure of a story. There is a beginning, a middle, and an end. There is usually a problem that happens in the beginning, the characters try to fix the problem in the middle, and in the end they either solve the problem (a happy ending) or they don't (a not-so-happy ending).

And just like how stories have happy or not-so-happy endings, stories have the power to be used for good or for not-so-good. They have this power because our brains are wired to receive, process, and store information we receive through stories in a deeper and more permanent way. That's why it's so dangerous to internalize the Trans Narrative.

The Trans Narrative tells trans and nonbinary people how they should behave, treat others, exist in public, obtain medical care, dress . . . all with the goal of making cisgender people as comfortable in our presence as possible. By removing all power from the trans or nonbinary person to make those decisions for themselves, it erases their authenticity and never prioritizes their desires or happiness.

Any story that is told to devalue another person, to tell them how they should live to be loved and accepted by others, is a terrible story indeed. That's why we are telling you about it now, so you can be ready when you start feeling other people trying to impose the Trans Narrative on you.

The History of the Modern Trans Narrative

Before we discuss where the modern Trans Narrative came from, let's remind ourselves that trans and nonbinary people have been around for all of human history. Just because the Trans Narrative is an oppressive thing now, doesn't mean that trans and nonbinary people's stories have always been negative. Throughout history and in many cultures, trans and nonbinary people were revered and respected for their insight and understanding of the fuller spectrum of human experience.

The modern Trans Narrative is largely an invention of the 20th century. With the advent of medical interventions for trans and nonbinary people, high-profile public figures were able to very visibly traverse the gender binary. Christine Jorgensen was the first widely known transgender person in the United States, being profiled by the media at length after her gender confirmation surgery in Denmark in the early 1950s. Christine had been very visibly "male" and had become very visibly "female," and cisgender people were taken aback. Cis people expected all trans and non-binary people to follow in her footsteps. But for people with less privilege, being able to socially and medically transition in a way that afforded them the ability to "pass" was simply out of reach.

With the public's interest in trans people piqued, American pop culture rose to meet the demand for stories about people who transgressed the gender binary. Daytime TV shows of the '80s and '90s depicted trans women (and sometimes trans men) as oddities as a way to increase their ratings. Often, these portrayals were negative and mocked the trans experience by implying that trans  people who didn't pass were not "trans enough" and should be relegated to the shadows of society. In the worst cases, these shows used cis men who were poorly cross dressed to further reinforce the idea that trans women were nothing more than "men in dresses." Trans men, when featured, were confused and conflated with lesbians, and nonbinary people were not featured at all.

How the Trans Narrative Plays Out

The Trans Narrative's elements vary depending on whether we're talking about trans women, trans men, or nonbinary people. But the purpose of the Trans Narrative is always the same—it imposes a set of criteria on trans and nonbinary people to minimize the discomfort of cisgender people. The Trans Narrative is toxic because it implies that the only valid way for trans and nonbinary people to exist in the world is to make cisgender people more comfortable. As with most kinds of oppression, the Trans Narrative was created and is furthered by the dominant group (cisgender people), but the minority group can also further it among themselves. This can happen when trans people tell each other that they are not "trans enough." The medical community also specifically contributes to the Trans Narrative through protocols and standards of care that determine what types of medical care are available and when.

We'll start by examining the Trans Narrative and how it is applied to trans women, because the narrative was developed with them in mind. Then we'll touch on how the Trans Narrative is applied to trans men and nonbinary people.

The homogenous Trans+ Narrative that is so widely disseminated through our culture and society today nearly defeats the entire purpose of a narrative. Narratives exist to tell personal stories, to bring stories, thoughts, and interactions to life for an audience who may never have the opportunity to experience them. The standardization of narratives disrespects the diversity and individuality of a group's members.

Hearing the same, largely untrue story over and over and over is boring and it's not doing us any favors. Discussions of trans+ people are always centered around a male-female binary, and all of the stories are the same. Person starts questioning their identity, they realize they're trans, they begin to experiment with dressing in "opposite-gender" clothing, they experience crippling dysphoria, they move through their coming out process, they are ostracized by their community, they find home, but still bear the scars of their struggles. While people do experience these things, and while I don't mean to discount anyone's experiences, this is not what all of us go through, and this narrative is incredibly harmful to all of those whose lives may not fit within it.

Nonbinary people, genderqueer people, gender-fluid people, gender-nonconforming people, agender people, bigender people, demigender people, and others whose identities cannot be categorized as strictly male or female are harmed when they only hear narratives that don't include them. It took me a long time to identify as trans+, because, though I knew I wasn't cis, I didn't believe I fit in the trans+ community.

Thankfully, it seems more and more people are recognizing that a shift in this narrative is essential to ensuring the trans+ community can be seen as a safe and accepting place for everyone. I still struggle with feeling like I am not trans+ enough, but knowing there are nonbinary people who identify as trans+ has helped a lot.

E.

The Trans Narrative and Trans Women

For trans women, the Trans Narrative usually starts with the concept of a countdown clock. The idea is that as soon as a trans woman comes out, a clock starts counting down from two years; when the clock reaches zero, she should be "stealth" (a trans person who is read as a cisgender person at all times and has ended contact with anyone who knew them pre-transition), or at the very least "passable."

During this period, a trans woman is expected to:

- complete all the necessary therapy to get letters in support of her desired medical transition procedures (HRT, surgeries, etc.);

- socially transition to living full time as a woman;

- buy a whole new wardrobe and get rid of all of her "male" clothes;

- purchase and learn to flawlessly apply makeup;

- save up, schedule, and complete "THE surgery";

- destroy all evidence of her previous life (burning baby pictures, moving to a new city, changing jobs, etc.).

This timeline probably seems really fast and nearly unattainable, but that's the point. Two years seems to be about as fast as it is possible for any person to get all of these things done, which is why that's the general expectation.

You'll notice that all of these things sound pretty hard and lonely, and that none of these things are done with the trans woman's desires at the forefront. Yes, she's come out, but the imposed timeline and the prescribed steps are all part of the Narrative's reinforcement of the idea that trans women will only be acceptable in society if they are indistinguishable from cisgender women. This stems from society's expectation that AMAB people (those who were assigned a male sex at birth) should rarely (preferably never) express any feminine-of-center interests, behaviors, or attitudes. An AMAB kid dressing in girls' clothes, and playing with girls' toys is not tolerated in most cultures and families in the United States. There is so little room for children to experiment and try on different forms of gender expression and identity. It's why trans women are expected to do all of their exploration and transitioning in private.

The other, overarching part of the Trans Narrative for trans women is this insistence that they had to have ALWAYS known that they were "trapped in the wrong body." That somehow not knowing from their first awareness of their gender that they were trans makes their identities invalid. This is simply not true. No matter why or when a person comes to understand their gender identity, it is valid.

The Trans Narrative and Trans Men

For trans men, the Trans Narrative plays out a bit differently, but the expectation to be "stealth" or at the very least "passing" for the comfort of cisgender people remains.

Whereas gender roles for AMAB people are strictly enforced, AFAB people (those who were assigned a female sex at birth) tend to have a little more leeway in expressing their gender in ways that aren't considered "typical." The most recognizable example of this is the concept of "tomboys"—AFAB people who have more

I came out as transgender at the age of 17. It wasn't the first time I'd heard of transgender people, the first time I questioned my gender, or even the first time I thought I was transgender. Growing up, I was always interested in LGBTQ+ people, especially transgender people. As someone who was assigned female at birth (AFAB) but grew up playing zombie tag with the boys and wouldn't be caught dead seeming feminine, when I heard about people whose gender didn't match their genitals, my first thought was, "Am I like that?" So I read all the books I could, every memoir and autobiography I could find in the library, and concluded that I could not possibly be transgender. Every time, a few years would pass, I would wonder again, and read in the books a definitive no. Everyone had different experiences, but they all told the same story: they knew from the time they were three, didn't understand why others couldn't see it, expected puberty to give them the body they always knew they should have had, never understood why they had to change themselves to fit others' expectations, fought for love and bodies that felt right to them, came out, had a hard time, everyone finally accepted them, they transitioned, and then they were good. As I grew up, others would ask me sometimes, too: "Are you transgender?" And I always told them, "No way! Those people know they're in the wrong body as toddlers, and that's not me. I'm just a tomboy." When I got older, YouTube exploded with sex-positive LGBTQ+ vloggers talking openly about their experiences, and that's when I started to get the idea that there could be all kinds of transgender people, even in the binary sense. I became even more intrigued by nonbinary identities, like neutrois and gender-fluid, and I began to question one last time. What finally did it for me was the day I came across a short blurb explaining what the Trans Narrative was. It finally occurred to me that no one story can define any group of people, and the fact that it wasn't my story did not disqualify me. Gradually, I learned to accept that I was a different kind of transgender. Imagine my shock when I joined a GSA full of other high school students who had the exact same experience as me!

Tai

As trans people, I feel like most of us remember what it was like to learn about what transitioning was from an outsider perspective. I remember seeing a news story on TV when I was young about a man who transitioned to a woman, and then back to a man later in life. This was the first time I learned someone could change genders from the one they were assigned at birth, and the idea was something I had never been exposed to before. I remember how the narration framed it as if he had made the biggest mistake of his life, and had only realized it when he was older. Looking back on trans representation in media when I was growing up, a lot of it involved cases like this, where the idea of transitioning was shunned, or seen as the punchline of a joke, as if any self-respecting person wouldn't dare attempt such a feat. I didn't think any less of trans people because of these ideas, but it did make me afraid to experiment with my own gender in any way, for fear of being treated like the people I saw on TV. From what I had seen portrayed in the media, it felt like I was being taught that trans people couldn't live normal lives, and were deemed outcasts because of it. It wasn't until I was much older, and a friend showed me a YouTube channel run by a trans woman who talked about her experiences, that I realized being trans doesn't mean you can't function as a normal human being. Seeing her live her life and thrive really opened the door for me to reconsider my own gender identity and, ultimately, decide to transition. I truly feel that if trans people were given a platform like this more often, uneducated people would begin to realize being trans doesn't make you any different than anyone else, and I feel like exposure to these ideas would release the stigma around trans people that some people currently harbor.

masculine-of-center interests, behaviors, and attitudes. Tomboys are often allowed to wear more "boyish" clothes and may even be allowed to get more "masculine" haircuts without cultural judgment. Of course, the underlying assumption is usually that the tomboy is just "going through a phase" and will grow out of their tomboyishness. When they don't grow out of it by the time they reach puberty, it might then be assumed they are or will become a lesbian. Trans men who were labeled tomboys growing up might experience confusion in trying to understand their gender identity. Because they were able to express the gender identity a little more openly, it may create an internal struggle to understand the difference between their sexuality and gender identity.

Kathryn

I attempted to transition four times and stopped each time. It wasn't until my fifth attempt that I was successful. Why did I "change my mind" so many times? Because I felt like I wasn't going to be able to live up to the daunting expectations that are placed on trans women like me by the Trans Narrative.

I didn't feel like I would ever be "trans enough" or "woman enough," because I couldn't or didn't want to do the things the Narrative requires. This led to some pretty terrible dysphoria and imposter syndrome that took a long time to get over.

Thankfully, my awesome therapist stuck with me and, over time, we deconstructed the Narrative and I discovered how I wanted my transition to go. I'm so thankful I was able to escape the Narrative's evil clutches and make a story that is all my own.

The Trans Narrative and Nonbinary People

For nonbinary people, the Trans Narrative hasn't really caught up with them enough to impose one set of strict criteria to follow, but the general expectation to avoid making cisgender people uncomfortable is certainly present. In some ways, this expectation is even more pronounced because at the core of cisgender people's need for comfort is the desire for trans and nonbinary people to appear as cisgender and conform to typical binary gender roles. Because nonbinary people often seek to exist outside of the binary, their non-conformity is especially threatening to cis people. This leads people who adhere to the gender binary to pressure nonbinary people to "just pick one" gender and stick with it.

Of course, we know this is silly. Nonbinary people did pick one—they picked to be themselves and that just happens to be outside the binary. Again, other people's comfort should not dictate how you exist in the world.

Breaking Down the Trans Narrative

The first step to breaking down any spoken or unspoken assumptions is to challenge them—if it is safe to do so—when they arise. One of the best ways to challenge someone's assumptions is to ask them questions. When you approach a person with the intent to understand where they're coming from (even when the place they are coming from is *really, really dumb*), it helps you understand what exactly they are assuming and how you might want to proceed.

Given that the Trans Narrative is largely about dictating the speed and the outcome of a person's transition, another great way to break down the Narrative is to go at your own speed and define your goals based on what you know to be best for you.

In the end, the best way to dismantle the Trans Narrative is to ignore it and live your life. Be you and be happy. Nothing is going to break down the oppressive nature of the Narrative more than doing what is best for you and living your best life. And when you've broken the Narrative, make sure to tell your story to other people so they know it's possible.

What Makes You Say That?

A great general question to ask is: "What makes you say that?" When asked in a neutral tone, it invites the other person to lay out their line of thinking for you. From there, you can decide if it's worth your time to continue engaging with them.

Cis person: "Why can't you just be a boy or a girl? I just think you should pick one."

Nonbinary person: "What makes you say that?"

Cis person: "Well . . . umm . . . ?

Nonbinary person: "It's okay. I'd really like to know what makes you say that."

Cis person: "Hmm . . . well . . . I guess I hadn't thought about it. I think I keep asking you to pick one gender or the other because it would be easier for me to understand."

Nonbinary person: " . . . "

Cis person: " . . . "

Nonbinary person: "So, if I'm understanding you correctly, you're asking me, a nonbinary person, to pick a binary gender identity so you can be more comfortable when we hang out for a few hours each week?"

Cis person: "YES! I'm so glad you understand!"

Nonbinary person: "And I'm so sad that you don't."

Additional Resources

thetransbook.com/link/0601
This is a great place to learn about the wide variety and beauty of the life stories of trans and nonbinary people.

thetransbook.com/link/0602
Nobody Passes: Rejecting the Rules of Gender and Conformity
by Matt Bernstein Sycamore (Editor)

thetransbook.com/link/0603
Finding Masculinity: Female to Male Transition in Adulthood
by Alexander Walker and Emmett J.P. Lundberg

thetransbook.com/link/0604
Trans Bodies, Trans Selves
by Laura Erickson-Schroth

thetransbook.com/link/0605
Black on Both Sides: A Racial History of Trans Identity
by C. Riley Snorton

thetransbook.com/link/0606
Born on the Edge of Race and Gender: A Voice for Cultural Competency
by Willy Wilkinson

CHAPTER 7

SOCIAL TRANSITION

here is no one right way to express your trans or nonbinary identity. It's something you'll experiment with and change over time as you come to know yourself better and better. That said, there are a few pretty standard ways to achieve the gender expression you want for yourself. Whether it's your clothes, hair, or voice, or taking the step to bind your chest or tuck— how you express your wonderful, beautiful self is all up to you.

Let's Talk About Passing

"Passing" is a term used to describe a trans or nonbinary person whose gender expression allows them to be perceived as the gender they identify as, and for binary trans people, to such an extent that they are assumed to be cisgender.

We talked about passing a lot in Chapter 6 in the context of the Trans Narrative. It is problematic for cisgender people to expect trans and nonbinary people to conform to a specific set of gender standards. At the same time, passing is a way to try and ensure your physical and emotional safety in your daily life (even if the gender expression you present that allows you to pass is different from your internal sense of your gender identity).

People around you will give you feedback (even if you don't want it) about whether you are passing or not. They might do this through words ("OMG! I would have never guessed you were trans!" #eyeroll) or through actions (a person at the mall gives you major side eye).

Positive feedback about your gender expression will probably feel really good, and negative feedback will feel really bad (and might even make you feel unsafe). People pass in different ways at different times with different people around. Don't judge other trans or nonbinary people for how much they do or don't pass, or if they do or don't want to pass. It's up to each of us to determine how we want to exist in the world each day. It hurts people when they are told they should, or must, pass in order to be trans. Whether you pass or not, it doesn't invalidate your transness, just like whether another trans or nonbinary person passes or not doesn't invalidate theirs.

How to Trans

There is no one right way to be trans. Your job is to make you feel as much like yourself as possible (while also making sure you are safe)! Usually, the goal in trying to figure out how to express your gender is to prevent coming out when you didn't intend to or being forced out by circumstances beyond your control.

Some of the ways you can signal your gender identity to others are through your name and pronouns, the clothes you wear, how your hair is cut and styled, what your voice sounds like, your mannerisms, certain medical interventions, and changing your legal identification documents. As part of your gender expression, you may also choose to bind your chest or tuck your genitals.

Name and Pronouns

One of the first places trans and nonbinary people start their social transition is by choosing a name, which can be a fun but sometimes overwhelming process. There are many websites that can help you research the meaning of names, but at a certain point, you might feel paralyzed by the number of names you like. If you have supportive friends or family members, ask them to help you "try on" a name by using it for a day. Check in with yourself and see how it feels. If it's comfortable and makes you feel like you, it's probably a good name to consider! If not, then try on a different name the next day or the next week until you find something that fits.

At this stage, trans and nonbinary people also tend to decide on the pronouns they will use. There are many different kinds of pronouns and you may need to try them on for a minute to see what works best for you. You also have the right to change your pronouns when they no longer suit you, just like your name.

Gender Pronouns

This is not a comprehensive list of pronouns, but should give you a place to start. To understand how to use each one, insert the pronoun from the corresponding letter into the sample sentences below. It's like a Pronouns-by-Numbers!

Subject: [1] believes gender is a beautiful spectrum, not a binary.

Object: They tried to convince [2] that nonbinary people should just pick a gender.

Possessive: [3] favorite book is *TRANS+*.

Possessive Pronoun: That nonbinary flag pin is [4].

Reflexive: [1] is always saying wonderful and amazing things about [5].

Subjective [1]	Objective [2]	Possessive [3]	Possessive Pronoun [4]	Reflexive [5]
ae	aer	aer	aers	aerself
e/ey	em	eir	eirs	eirself
fae	faer	faer	faers	faerself
he	him	his	his	himself
per	per	pers	pers	perself
she	her	her	hers	herself
they	them	their	theirs	themself
ve	ver	vis	vis	verself
xe	xem	xyr	xyrs	xemself
ze/zie	hir	hir	hirs	hirself

Clothing

Clothing is often the easiest way to get started with expressing your gender, whether you're in public or in private. If you've come out to close friends, a great way to get started without having to have money is to try on your friends' clothes! This will give you an idea of what feels good and looks good on you.

When it's time to start building your own wardrobe, there are a few things to keep in mind:

- Are my parents going to be supportive of my desire to have new clothes and to wear them in public?
- If not, what will I do if my parents find out I'm wearing clothes that match my gender identity?
- If I need to, where can I hide my clothes so my parents don't find them?
- Where am I going to get my clothes and how am I going to pay for them?
- Will I be safe wearing the clothes I want to school and in public?

Based on your answers to these questions, you might decide to wear your new clothes only in private, only at home, only at school, etc. You can check-in about your answers to them every few months to see if things have changed.

Hair

Hair is a relatively easy way to express your gender identity, though this one is hard to keep private! The biggest problem trans and nonbinary people have, especially youth, in getting the haircuts they want is finding a stylist who will actually listen to what they want their hair to look like. AFAB youth often complain about going to the barbershop and asking for a masculine haircut, only to be given something more feminine than they wanted, while AMAB youth have a similar experience (in reverse) at salons.

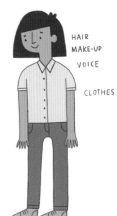

HAIR
MAKE-UP
VOICE

CLOTHES

A great way to address this problem is to ask around to see if other trans or nonbinary people can recommend a stylist that will actually listen and give you the haircut you want. You should also bring pictures of what you want your hair to look like. This will give the stylist a good indication of what you want.

You'll need to be willing to speak up if the haircut you get isn't what you want. If you brought pictures, you can refer back to them and explain how the haircut you've been given doesn't match and ask them to keep going until it looks like the picture. If not, try to be as specific as possible when you're explaining why you are disappointed with your hairstyle.

Karen

Hair can also be a hugely fun element of expression. Starting with The Beatles in the '60s (Hair that touched their collars! Oh my!), hair culture in the United States has become increasingly fluid with all kinds of alternatives. There are often more fluid options with hair length, color, and style than other areas of your gender expression. There are even some haircuts that can look both quite feminine and quite masculine, depending on how they're styled, which would allow for flexibility depending on how you're feeling or who you're with that day. A good stylist—and definitely one who is accustomed to cutting hair for trans and nonbinary people—would ideally talk these things through with you.

Makeup

Makeup, like clothes, is an easy way to experiment with your gender expression and, just like clothes, a great place to start is by asking a supportive friend to help you put on makeup for the first (or second or third) time. This will give you a good idea of what look you are going for and help you create a list of products and supplies you'll need to copy the look on your own. If you don't have a friend who can help you, YouTube is a great place to go to learn all about makeup application and skincare.

Again, as with clothes, you'll need to keep some things in mind as you build your makeup kit:

- Are my parents going to be supportive of my desire to wear makeup at home? What about in public?

- Where am I going to get my makeup and how am I going to pay for it?
- If I need to, where can I hide my makeup so my parents don't find it?
- What will I do if my parents find out I'm wearing makeup and they're not supportive?
- Will I be safe wearing makeup to school and out in public?

Just like with clothes, you might decide to wear your new makeup only in private, only at home, only at school, etc. You can check-in about your answers to them every few months to see if things have changed.

Voice

Voice is one of the harder things to change about gender expression. For AMAB people to raise the pitch of their voice once it has dropped, they will either need to do voice training and/or get vocal cord surgery. For AFAB people, testosterone will lower the pitch of their voice. But if you are not yet on testosterone, or don't plan to be, you can also do voice training.

No matter what you want your voice to sound like, there are many great YouTube videos and apps available to help you get there. Check out the resources section at the end of this chapter.

Kathryn

My voice is the one place I didn't spend much time focusing on. To me, there were so many other things I needed to worry about that researching voice modification methods or finding a voice coach to help me "feminize" my voice was more than I could handle. That said, I don't know what's happened over time. I watch old videos of myself and my voice has definitely changed—it's probably still in a "male" range, but I get gendered correctly on the phone 99% of the time. It's been nice to know my voice finally caught up with me all these years later. It may not be that feminine, but it's mine, and I love it. I hope you grow to find your voice and love it too!

I'd say social transitioning is the most misunderstood part about transition as a whole, because it's something that begins the moment you come out to yourself as trans. When I realized I was a boy, I almost immediately had to adjust my brain to using he/him pronouns for myself, and looked at a bunch of names to replace my deadname. Social transitioning is shifting the way you live, the way you interact with people, often times the way  you dress and express yourself, to better suit how you feel. When I came out to more and more people, I noticed it was easier for me to be seen as a dude as I shifted how I spoke and how I carried my body language. It's the smallest visual and audio cues that change how people see you in social settings. The funniest thing I noticed was, after coming out, I actually started manspreading and taking up a little more space when I sat down. I know people hate that, but I found it funny that I adopted that habit after shifting my mannerisms to more masculine ones. Even my ways of expressing affection changed as the way I spoke had changed. I still say "I love you" to my friends, but compared to a lot of my female friends, it's more of a "love you, bro" than a long proclamation, if that makes sense. All of this came long before any medical or legal transitioning, and it's the most long-lasting of all forms of gender transition, which I find incredibly amazing. Your name, the way you act, and the way you conduct yourself are the first things that get to reflect who you are inside.

Luka

Chest Binding

Binding is the process of compressing the chest tissue to achieve a flatter, more masculine appearance of the torso, and decrease chest dysphoria. There are many ways to bind the chest, each with their own safety and comfort concerns. There are some great resources at the end of this chapter that go into greater detail on the various ways to bind how to keep yourself as safe as possible.

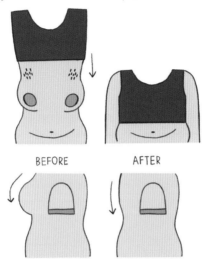

BEFORE   AFTER

There are companies that sell chest binders that are made of a special compression material that flatten the chest and help minimize (but not eliminate) the safety and health concerns associated with binding. They tend to be the most expensive option, but they are considered the most effective.

Other ways people bind their chest include:

- tape
- bandages
- layered clothing
- compression garments
- neoprene braces
- control-top pantyhose

Each of these methods has its pros and cons as far as cost, efficacy, and safety. Tape may be inexpensive and easy to find, but the adhesive in the tape can cause skin irritation and make it hard to breathe because the tape doesn't stretch. Bandages are also an option discussed a lot due to their affordability, but most bandages, especially ace bandages, are designed to get tighter as you move around, which can hurt your ribs and make it hard to breathe.

No matter how you bind, listen to your body and take note of any bruising, soreness, redness, itchiness, swelling, chest tightness, or trouble breathing.

Tucking

Tucking is the process of tucking the penis back and between the legs to produce a flat appearance in the genital region. The testicles are either tucked back as well or pushed up into the abdomen. There are some great resources at the end of this chapter that go into greater detail on the various ways to tuck and how to keep yourself as safe as possible.

There are many ways to tuck:
- tape
- a special garment called a gaff
- shapewear (like Spanx)
- tight underwear (usually combined with shapewear)

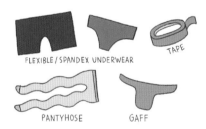

FLEXIBLE / SPANDEX UNDERWEAR

TAPE

PANTYHOSE

GAFF

You may do all, some, or none of these depending on the kind of appearance you want to achieve. There are some great You-Tube videos in the resources section at the end of this chapter that go into tucking with tape, making your own gaff at home, or achieving a comfortable tuck with tight underwear and shapewear.

Like chest binding, there are some health and safety risks to be aware of when you tuck. Prolonged tucking, no matter the method, can negatively impact your fertility (the ability for your body to produce the gamete cells we talked about in Chapter 5). There's also the risk of skin irritation from repeated contact with the adhesive in tape, or fungal infections from having your bits (which tend to be moist) all tucked up for hours on end.

No matter how you tuck, listen to your body and take note of any bruising, soreness, redness, itchiness, swelling, or change in odor.

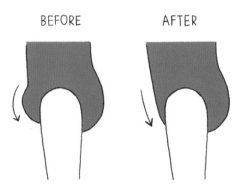

BEFORE   AFTER

Packing

Packing is the wearing of padding or a phallic object to give the appearance of having a bulge in the genital area. There are two primary ways to pack: creating a homemade packer (using socks, stockings, condoms, and other materials) or purchasing a packer. We've included links at the end of this chapter on ways to make your own packer and packing underwear at home, as well as some places where you can purchase a packer and packing underwear online.

When purchasing a packer, there are various kinds to choose from:
- regular packers
- STP (stand-to-pee) packers
- pack and play packers
- combinatin of the above

Given all of the options and features you can find in packers, it might be tempting to go with the most expensive option, but sometimes an inexpensive packer will be just as comfortable and realistic. Select a packer that you're likely to wear on a daily basis.

Packing underwear is just as, if not more important than the packer you choose. The right kind of underwear will help keep the packer in position, which provides comfort during long periods of wear as well as safety (it keeps the packer from falling out when going to the restroom for example). Again, price doesn't necessarily indicate quality. There are specially-designed underwear for packing which are great, but you can also find sheath pouch underwear online (which also work great for swimming) for an affordable price.

To prolong the life of your packer and to keep your skin and genitals healthy, make sure you clean your packer daily. Also, it's best not to sleep with your packer on as your body needs to breathe overnight to prevent the growth of bacteria.

Learning how to start feeling comfortable with who I am has been tough, and I'm still far from having it all figured out. Though I thoroughly enjoy both traditionally feminine and masculine things, I have found that distancing myself as much as possible from the feminine identity I have lived with for the last fifteen years has helped me to feel much more comfortable moving through the world as a nonbinary person.

Though dresses are fun and, honestly, I don't hate them, I refuse to wear them because I feel much more confident in masculine clothing. For me, masculinity helps provide some sense of balance; rather than wear the things that one would expect to correspond with the female body in which I was born, I'll wear some sagging pants, a button-up shirt, and a snapback. Non-conformity makes me feel more comfortable in my body, because, though I have a hard time getting people to accept that I do not identify as female, I can at least get them to accept that I dress like a boy.

Experimenting has helped me a lot as well. I spend so much time in front of the mirror changing the way I walk, changing the way I wear my clothes, changing the way I stand, changing the way I sit, changing the way I talk, changing the way I laugh, just changing little things about myself so I can more accurately reflect my identity.

Transitioning is all a huge learning curve, and there is no one-size-fits-all way of doing it. My best advice would be to just try everything, because sometimes the smallest things make the biggest difference. I was awestruck by how much better I liked the way my clothes fit once I started binding. Asking to be referred to by they/them pronouns made me so much less uncomfortable when people talked about me in the third person. Being trans+ is hard, but there are so many little things that can be done to make it easier.

E.

Additional Resources

thetransbook.com/link/0701
This is a great resource from GC2B, a company that makes chest binders, on Binder Basics like binder fitting, binder care, and binder safety.

thetransbook.com/link/0702
Point5cc is a trans-owned company that has a great Binder 101 section on their website with links to binder donation programs where you can apply to get a free binder!

thetransbook.com/link/0703
TransGuys.com has a great list of all the places you can shop for a binder or get one donated.

thetransbook.com/link/0704
Stacy Fatemi is a nonbinary person and YouTuber who made a video on tucking, especially using stuff that's easy to find around the house or at the grocery store.

thetransbook.com/link/0705
Princess Joules is a trans woman and YouTuber who did this great tutorial on tucking for when you wear swimsuits.

thetransbook.com/link/0706
Alayna June is a trans woman and YouTuber who discusses tucking more comfortably.

thetransbook.com/link/0707
ReelMagik offers lightweight and affordable packers in a variety of form factors and skin tones.

thetransbook.com/link/0708
This video by uppercaseCHASE1 explains packing for youth. The video also addresses questions parents might have about packing.

thetransbook.com/link/0709
This video by MackMan explains how you can make your own packing underwear.

thetransbook.com/link/0710
This video by Snapbacks and Bowties explains how you can make a very simple packer out of socks.

thetransbook.com/link/0711
This video by Jay'sJourney—FtM has tips for beginners on packing.

CHAPTER 8

MEDICAL TRANSITION

Transgender and gender-nonbinary people often, but not always, pursue medical treatments to further their transition beyond what is possible socially. Medical treatment options can include hormone blockers, hormone replacement therapy, gender-affirming surgeries, and other interventions that help bring a person's body into alignment with who they know themselves to be.

This chapter will explore and expand on all kinds of medical treatment options, discuss the changes to the body that can be expected with hormone treatments, and offer suggestions on how youth can discuss their medical goals with their families and medical providers.

It is important to understand, especially as you do your own research, that much of the information you will find was created by non-trans people for other non-trans people. It can be really uncomfortable reading something about trans bodies that was written for cis people. Be gentle with yourself and seek out resources that feel right for you

Making the Decision

Medical transition is not a requirement to identify as transgender or gender-nonbinary. Whether you've not started medical treatments or chosen not to pursue medical transition, your identity is valid just as you are.

There are many reasons someone might not pursue medical transition. They might not have the financial resources or insurance that covers transition-related care. Sometimes a person has other medical conditions that prevent them from taking hormones or having any kind of surgery. And for some trans and nonbinary people, they simply don't want any kind of medical transition because their dysphoria is social, not physical.

Just like coming out, making the decision to start medical transition should be a process of coming to understand if you want to medically transition, what you're wanting, what resources and options are available to you, and making sure you fully understand the benefits and drawbacks of the treatments you are pursuing. If you are a minor, you'll also need a parent or guardian to consent to these treatments for you.

A great way to think through this process is to create a list of things you are hoping to get from medically transitioning. Like we've said, if there's nothing you feel like you'd get out of medically transitioning, maybe socially transitioning is all you need. But if there are things you are excited about—like a deeper voice, hairless skin, or a sparkly new set of genitals—write those down. As you read through this chapter, see what procedures make the most sense for you. From there, you can create a timeline and a plan for achieving each of those steps.

For nonbinary youth, thinking through this process can be especially difficult because most medical transition procedures were developed to help trans people "cross the binary." To achieve their medical transition-related goals, nonbinary youth will have to be especially clear with their medical providers about just how far they want each of their changes to go.

For some AFAB people who are nonbinary, they may want to have chest surgery and make their voice deeper, but not want to grow facial or body hair. And for some AMAB people who are nonbinary, they may want smooth skin and some chest development, but not want to have genital surgery. All of these paths are valid and medical providers should be willing to help you achieve the goals you have for your body.

Once you make the decision to begin medical transition, you may encounter some barriers to getting the care you want. We talked about the gatekeeping model and informed consent model to care in Chapter 2. It's a good idea to familiarize yourself with the kinds of gatekeeping you might experience and understand the criteria you may be asked to meet in order to prove you are "trans enough" to your doctors and other medical providers. Remember: you are perfect exactly the way you are and there is no such thing as being "trans enough," it's just that doctors like to have someone else tell them it is okay to treat you.

Hormone Blockers

Sometimes called "puberty blockers," hormone blockers are medications that can be given to transgender and gender-nonbinary youth to stop puberty. They have been shown to reduce feelings of dysphoria and improve mental health.

What Do Hormone Blockers Do?

Hormone blockers stop the development of secondary sexual characteristics (like breast development) and menstrual periods for AFAB people, and a deepening voice and facial hair for AMAB people. Not only does this reduce dysphoria, it can prevent the need for surgeries to modify those characteristics later on in life.

The medication in hormone blockers is called gonadotropin-releasing hormone or GnRH analogs. You already have GnRH inside you. It is produced by the hypothalamus gland in your brain and it is responsible for telling your pituitary gland to start the changes associated with puberty by sending luteinizing hormones and follicle stimulating hormones to the ovaries or testicles. The GnRH analog in hormone blockers stops the pituitary from sending out these hormones, which prevents the changes associated with puberty.

When Can You Start Hormone Blockers?

Typically, a doctor would begin hormone blockers when you begin puberty. For people assigned female at birth, this is usually between the ages of 9 and 14. For people assigned male at birth, this is usually between ages 10 and 20. Because these are such wide ranges in ages, it will be important for your doctor to determine your Tanner Stage of Development before deciding whether hormone blockers are a good choice for you.

The Tanner Stages of Development break down puberty into five stages. Chapter 4 has a great visual breakdown of each of these stages. Stage 1 is pre-puberty when no changes have happened to the body. Stage 2 and 3 are the beginning of puberty before secondary sexual characteristics develop and usually the stages at which a doctor would start prescribing hormone blockers. Stage 4 and 5 are late puberty, when it is more appropriate for a doctor to prescribe hormone replacement therapy.

When Should I Stop Hormone Blockers?

The decision to stop hormone blockers should be made with your doctor, as each person's situation will be different. It is entirely possible that your doctor would keep you on hormone blockers even after you start hormone replacement therapy to give you a puberty that is consistent with your gender identity. At this time, there is no consensus among medical providers at what age or stage of development it is appropriate to stop administering hormone blockers, but some will continue into late adolescence or early adulthood.

If you were to stop hormone blockers before starting hormone replacement therapy, puberty would continue where it left off and you would develop the secondary sex characteristics consistent with the sex you were assigned at birth.

Are There Risks to Taking Hormone Blockers?

The longer you stay on hormone blockers, the higher the risk there is to have medical complications like decreased bone density, weight gain, irregular moods, and emotional reactions. It is also possible that your body will never create fully mature gametes later in life.

Depending on if or when you choose to begin hormone replacement therapy, there's also the complication of having delayed puberty for years—meaning you would look significantly younger than your peers. There's also the difficulty of going through puberty at 15 or 16 years old instead of 11 or 12.

Weigh these risks against the benefits of hormone blockers and think through what it would be like to go through puberty later than your friends.

At the moment, I have little desire to go through the medical transition process. I don't know who I am yet, I'm still figuring a lot of things out, and I'm not secure enough in my identity to know what I would want. I think these decisions become especially difficult for people who identify outside of the gender binary, because there's not an expectation for what a nonbinary person would look like. In society, we expect women to have breasts, long hair, and a vagina, and we expect men to have flat chests, short hair, and a penis. But what does a nonbinary person look like?

I know it will probably be a long time before I decide if and when I want to medically transition in any way. More and more, I'm starting to realize that this is really a personal decision, and the idea that every trans+ person wants to transition can go to hell. Realizing that I do not have to medically transition or even want to transition to consider myself part of the trans+ community is definitely a process, but it's helping me on my journey to finding who I am.

E.

Hormone Replacement Therapy

Hormone replacement therapy (HRT) is a medical treatment in which a doctor prescribes hormones and other medications to help align a person's secondary sex characteristics with their gender identity.

Hormones are chemicals produced in the body to tell other cells how to develop. They have an effect on everything from blood sugar and metabolism to body fat and hair. By introducing new kinds of hormones, the body begins to change to match the signals it is getting.

What Does Hormone Replacement Therapy Do?

Hormone replacement therapy will do different things depending on whether you are seeking to feminize or masculinize your secondary sex characteristics.

Feminizing hormones (estrogens and anti-androgens) are used by transgender women and transfeminine people to increase the amount of estrogen and decrease the amount of testosterone in the body.

- **Estrogen** is a feminizing hormone that is responsible for the development of typically female secondary sex characteristics like breast development and fat distribution.

- **Anti-androgens** are hormones used to lower the amount of testosterone in the body to a typically female level.

Masculinizing hormones (androgens) are used by transgender men and transmasculine people to increase the amount of testosterone in the body.

- **Androgens** (testosterone) are masculinizing hormones that are responsible for the development of typically male secondary sex characteristics like facial hair growth, deepening of the voice, and an increase in muscle mass.

What Changes Can I Expect?

In general, you can expect HRT to change your secondary sex characteristics to match your gender identity. These changes happen gradually over time, though you can expect the majority of changes to happen within the first two years of treatment. Here are lists of changes and their expected timelines for both feminizing and masculinizing hormones. These will provide you with a general idea of changes you may experience with HRT, but remember that they are averages and your body may respond differently.

Effects and Expected Time Course for Masculinizing Hormones

EFFECT	EXPECTED ONSET[1]	EXPECTED MAX. EFFECT[1]
Skin oiliness/acne	1-6 months	1-2 years
Facial/body hair growth	3-6 months	3-5 years
Scalp hair loss	> 12 months[2]	variable
Increased muscle mass/strength	6-12 months	2-5 years[3]
Body fat redistribution	3-6 months	2-5 years
Cessation of menses	2-6 months	n/a
Clitoral enlargement	3-6 months	1-2 years
Vaginal atrophy	3-6 months	1-2 years
Deepened voice	3-12 months	1-2 years

From "The Standards of Care, 7th Version," by The World Professional Association for Transgender Health (WPATH), p. 37, Copyright 2012 by author. Reprinted with permission.

1. Estimates represent published and unpublished clinical data.
2. Highly dependend on age and inheritance; may be minimal.
3. Significantly dependent on amount of exercise.

The amount and speed of changes will depend on the dose of HRT you are taking, how you are taking your HRT, and the kind of HRT you are using, as well as your personal characteristics (how old you are, medical conditions you have, your overall health habits, etc.).

Effects and Expected Time Course of Feminizing Hormones

EFFECT	EXPECTED ONSET[4]	EXPECTED MAX. EFFECT[4]
Body fat redistribution	3-6 months	2-5 years
Decreased muscle mass/ strength	3-6 months	1-2 years[5]
Softening of the skin/ decreased oiliness	3-6 months	unknown
Decreased libido	1-3 months	1-2 years
Decreased spontaneous erections	1-3 months	3-6 months
Male sexual dysfunction	variable	variable
Breast growth	3-6 months	2-3 years
Decreased testicular volume	3-6 months	2-3 years
Decreased sperm production	variable	variable
Thinning and slowed growth of body and facial hair	6-12 months	> 3 years[6]
Male pattern baldness	no growth, loss stops 1-3 months	1-2 years

From "The Standards of Care, 7th Version," by The World Professional Association for Transgender Health (WPATH), p. 38, Copyright 2012 by author. Reprinted with permission.

---

4. Estimates represent published and unpublished clinical data.
5. Significantly dependent on amount of exercise.
6. Complete removal of male facial and body hair requires electrolysis, laser treatment, or both.

When Can I Start Hormone Replacement Therapy?

The age at which you can start HRT will depend on many factors, though most doctors currently start patients on hormones around age 16.

How Will I Take My Hormones?

The method you use to take your hormones will depend on the type of HRT you are taking, your particular needs, and any medical considerations.

Feminizing hormones are typically administered by pill, topical cream, or patches. You may even inject your feminizing hormones, though this is considered rare.

Masculinizing hormones are typically administered by injection. You may also administer your testosterone by topical cream or patches.

When Will I Stop Hormone Replacement Therapy?

Once you achieve the results you desire from HRT, usually after two years, you will continue on a maintenance dose for the rest of your life. Your maintenance dose is adjusted over time to account for changes in your health conditions, age, and other factors.

If you stop hormone replacement therapy altogether, you may begin developing the characteristics consistent with your sex assigned at birth.

What Are the Risks of Hormone Replacement Therapy?

As with all kinds of medical treatments, HRT has its risks. Your particular amount of risk will be determined based on the dose of HRT you are taking, how you are taking your HRT, and the kind of HRT you are using, as well as your personal characteristics (how old you are, medical conditions you have, your overall health habits, etc.).

The table on the next page, also from the WPATH Standards of Care, summarizes the risks and their severity for feminizing and masculinizing hormones.

Risks Association With Hormone Therapy. Bolded Items Are Clinically Significant.

Risk Level	Feminizing Hormones	Masculinizing Hormones
Likely increased risk	• **Venous thromboembolic disease**[7] • Gallstones • Elevated liver enzymes • Weight gain • **Hypertriglyceridemia**	• **Polycythemia** • Weight gain • Acne • Androgenic alopecia (balding) • Sleep apnea
Likely increased risk with presence of additional risk factors[8]	• Cardiovascular disease	
Possible increased risk	• **Hyptertension** • Hyperprolactinemia or prolactinom[7]	• Elevated liver enzymes • **Hyperlipidemia**
Possible increased risk with presence of additional risk factors[8]	• **Type 2 diabetes**[7]	• **Destabilization of certain psychiatric disorders**[9] • **Cardiovascular disease** • **Hypertension** • **Type 2 diabetes**
No increased risk or inconclusive	• **Breast cancer**	• Loss of bone density • **Breast cancer** • **Cervical cancer** • **Ovarian cancer** • **Uterine cancer**

From "The Standards of Care, 7th Version," by The World Professional Association for Transgender Health (WPATH), p. 40, Copyright 2012 by author. Reprinted with permission.

7. Risk is greater with oral estrogen administration than with transidermal estrogen administration.
8. Additional risk factors include age.
9. Includes bipolar, schizoaffective, and other disorders that may include psychotic symptoms. This adverse event appears to be associated with higher doses of supraphysiologic blood levels of testosterone.

Gender-Affirming Surgeries

Gender affirming surgeries give transgender and gender-nonbinary people the ability to have the appearance and abilities that conform to their gender identity.

Gender-Affirming Surgeries for Transfeminine People

- **Body feminization surgery** is a series of procedures performed using liposuction that contour the body into a more typically feminine shape when the changes from estrogen aren't enough.
- **Facial feminization surgery** changes typically masculine features of the face to typically feminine features and is done in one or more procedures.
- **Hair restoration surgery** creates a typically feminine hairline by transplanting hair from other areas of the head

into balding areas and may require several procedures to achieve full coverage.

- **Tracheal shaving** removes cartilage, known as the "Adam's Apple," to provide a more typically feminine appearance and is usually done in one procedure.
- **Transfeminine bottom surgery** reconstructs the penis into a vagina and is typically done in one procedure.
- **Transfeminine top surgery** enhances the shape and size of the breasts to create a typically feminine appearance and is usually done in one procedure.
- **Vocal feminization surgery** shortens the vocal cords to increase the pitch of the voice to a typically feminine range and is usually done in one procedure.

Gender-Affirming Surgeries for Transmasculine People

- **Body masculinization surgery** is a procedure performed using liposuction that contours the body into a more typically masculine shape when the changes from testosterone and top surgery aren't enough and may require several procedures to achieve the desired effect.
- **Facial masculinization surgery** changes typically feminine features of the face to typically masculine features and is done in one or more procedures.
- **Hysterectomy** is a one-time procedure that removes the uterus and cervix.
- **Metoidioplasty** is a procedure in which the ligament that holds the clitoris in place under the pubic bone is cut to free the clitoris from the surrounding tissue and bring it forward on the body to appear typically masculine and is usually done in one procedure.
- **Oophorectomy** is a procedure that removes both ovaries and both fallopian tubes and is usually performed as part of a hysterectomy.
- **Phalloplasty** is a procedure that creates a penis using tissue from other parts of the body and can be done in one or more procedures.
- **Transmasculine bottom surgery** is an umbrella term for a number of surgeries like metoidioplasty, phalloplasty, urethroplasty, and vaginectomy.

- **Transmasculine top surgery** removes the breast tissue to create a more typically masculine appearance and is usually done in one procedure.
- **Urethroplasty** is a procedure usually done during a metoidioplasty or phalloplasty that extends the urethra to the tip of the phallus.
- **Vaginectomy** is a procedure in which the mucosal lining of the vagina is removed and the walls are sutured together to eliminate the vagina and is usually done in one procedure.

How to Talk With Your Family and Doctors About Medical Transition

Talking about your goals for medical transition with your family and doctors can feel intimidating and scary. But there are great ways to make your needs known so you can feel more comfortable in your body.

Do Your Research

Educating yourself about the treatments you are interested in getting is a great way to show your family and doctors that you are serious about medical transition. One of the best places to find information is on surgeon's websites and on YouTube. Knowing the terminology, the specifics of procedures, and being realistic with yourself about the results can go a long way in showing maturity and encouraging adults to trust you in making these choices about your body.

As part of your research, you should also compile resources you want to share with your family and your doctors so they can study and answer their own questions as your medical transition continues.

Talk About the Benefits and How They Outweigh the Risks

One sure way to show you understand the seriousness of the procedures you are interested in getting is to be able to speak realistically and honestly about the risks. Nearly every medical procedure we've talked about in this chapter has some level of risk associated with it. By acknowledging that there is risk involved in your decisions, you can show you have given these procedures a lot of thought. You can also use your knowledge about the risks to explain how the benefits of the procedures outweigh the risks by making you more comfortable in your body, allowing you to focus less on dysphoria and more on school, and improving your overall mental health and body image.

Karen

It can be brutally hard to come to a deeply personal conversation with a logical, cool, clear head. Asking permission from your parents, which is what basically has to happen for a teenager to transition medically, with an even-keeled approach is asking a lot of anyone. I talk with parents of trans kids pretty often, and when their kid has come to them with a lot of information, research, and clear personal goals, the parents are usually able to come to acceptance and support of that process more quickly than when the kids are not as well organized. Hopefully the information in this chapter has gotten you at least part of the way toward being able to do that. A therapist or another trusted adult may be able to help you get the rest of the way there!

Admit What You Don't Know

"I don't know" can be one of the most powerful things you can say when discussing medical transition procedures with family and doctors. Making up answers to questions they ask you will only cause trouble down the line when the real answers come out. By admitting you don't know the answer, but that you'll do the research and get back to them, shows a level of maturity families and doctors are looking for to gauge your readiness for medical transition.

As someone who has always had a fear of drugs, beginning the medical transition process was pretty rough for me. I remember researching all through the night about the process of starting HRT, and what to expect when you finally begin. I remember reading about all of the benefits and getting so excited at the thought that I could experience the same thing. At the same time, something about it was still scary to me. The thought of any medication affecting things such as my emotional/ mental state always puts a pit in my stomach (it took me forever to work up the courage to take my ADD medication), and because of this, it was really hard for me to move forward with starting HRT. I was so worried that something that affects my mental state would somehow make me a different person, as if I would lose some part of who I am in the process. After some time, and a lot of working through my fear, I began the process of medically transitioning. As months passed and my estrogen levels went up, I did begin to notice changes in my emotional state. While my fears and insecurities were telling me that the changes would make me less of who I was, I had actually never felt more like myself. I've always been an emotional person but, for some reason, growing up it felt like my body wouldn't fully allow me to experience feelings like happiness or sadness. After starting HRT, I finally felt like I was experiencing these feelings, and the entire process felt more real to me, as if I had finally unlocked the full range of emotions I felt like I had always deserved to experience. In the end, I am really glad I faced my fears because it has made all the difference in my life, and finally I feel like I can truly experience the world the way I have always wanted to.

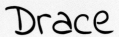

Drace

My relationship with medical treatment is tumultuous at best. Ever since I was 13 years old, I've wanted some form of medical transition, and at the forefront of that has always been testosterone hormone therapy. If you asked me today, right now as I write this, what my plans for medical transition are I wouldn't be able to tell you. It's difficult to fully grasp the idea of medical transition and what that would mean for me. Sometimes I wonder  whether or not I even want to go through with it, no matter how much I don't want to really look at myself in the mirror. It's difficult, and this idea that any trans person can follow this cookie-cutter, finite path to "fully transitioning" is, frankly, ridiculous. I know I personally don't know how I feel about getting bottom surgery, or if that's even something I feel would improve my life. What also throws a wrench into things is simply accessibility. It's hard for me to find sources on how hormone therapy would affect my current medical conditions, or how I could really start if I wanted to. How much everything costs varies constantly and I can't find enough reputable sources or research. Doctors, especially, that are specialized and safe for trans people to go to and talk about these kinds of changes are limited. It's complex, it feels like it always has been this complex, and I hope one day trans people can grow up and live as they want to without all these extra steps involved.

Luka

It's Your Body

Medical interventions are not required to prove your "transness." There are many reasons why a person would decide to delay or forego medical transition, but that does not negate their gender identity and who they know themselves to be.

Ultimately, your body is your own. If you're a minor, your parents and doctors may try to exert more control over your body (specifically what they don't want you to do). Thankfully, you will eventually turn 18 and be able to make your own decisions about your identity, your expression, and the medical steps you want to take to bring those into alignment.

Additional Resources

 thetransbook.com/link/0801
This is an amazing article about Hayley Anthony, a transgender woman who invented a new approach to vaginoplasty.

 thetransbook.com/link/0802
This article is a tough read, but gives a good sense about what people think about trans and nonbinary youth seeking medical interventions for transition. If you're preparing to talk with your parents or doctors about medical transition, this article might help you think of questions you can be ready to answer.

 thetransbook.com/link/0803
Provides a great overview of types of surgeries, sample letters, and post-surgical care advice.

thetransbook.com/link/0804
Provides a comprehensive overview of all kinds of medical interventions along with plenty of links to outside sources to explore. You could get lost in here for hours!

 thetransbook.com/link/0805
The mission of the Jim Collins Foundation is to provide financial assistance to transgender people for gender-confirming surgeries.

CHAPTER 9

LEGAL TRANSITION

The legal issues facing transgender and gender-nonbinary people are constantly evolving and vary based on where they are located geographically. You may choose to take legal actions to change your identity documents or challenge discrimination in the courts and other legal systems. These steps can be overwhelming, so take them in bits and chunks instead of all at once.

This chapter provides a basic overview of the kinds of legal steps you might take to change your identity, the kinds of discrimination you might encounter, ways to go about addressing your concerns in court, and ways to fight back against discrimination at school. The resources section in this chapter should be especially helpful in guiding you to the resources you need that apply to your location.

Disclaimer

We're not lawyers. That means we can't give you specific legal advice. You also shouldn't rely on this chapter as legal advice about the steps you are taking in your legal transition. You should reach out to organizations that specialize in helping transgender and gender-nonbinary people with legal transition issues. These organizations usually provide their help at low or no cost. You might also want to reach out to a lawyer that specializes in LGBTQIA+ law. Of course, lawyers will be more expensive, but they may be better skilled at helping you, especially if your needs are more complex.

Another thing to be aware of is that based on your geographic location and whether your parents are willing to help you and be supportive, these changes will be more or less difficult to achieve.

No matter how hard it gets, you know who you are, even if your identification documents don't reflect that. You are strong and capable and when you are 18, you can make these decisions and take actions for yourself.

Karen

I am a big proponent of people changing their names.

I was born with a different first and last name and changed them legally when I was 11 and 19, respectively. I made those changes because my name didn't fit with who I was and how I wanted to move through the world. I've lived more than half my life with my name now, and I still love it just as much as I did when I first chose it. I've advised a number of other people as they've picked out new first and last names for themselves. It's always a thrilling, personal, and empowering process.

My favorite thing I've ever read about a name is that it is a gift from a parent to a child. As with any gift from one person to another, if it doesn't fit, you should return it and pick out your own.

Potential Legal Steps & Issues

The steps of legal transition will vary person by person, but there are a few pretty common steps as well as some unfortunately difficult challenges you might face along the way.

Legal Name Change

This is the process of petitioning (making a formal request) a court to change your name legally. If the petition is approved, you can use the final order issued by the court to change your name on your driver's license, Social Security card, bank accounts, school records, and anywhere else it might show up in a legal context.

Sex/Gender Marker Change

This is the process of petitioning a court to change your sex/gender marker legally. (We have to say "sex/gender" because the law in many places still hasn't learned that there's a difference between the two.) If the petition is approved, you can use the final order issued by the court to change your sex and/or gender marker on your driver's license, with the Social Security office (even though it's not on your Social Security card), on school records, on medical records, and anywhere else it might show up in a legal context.

All the Places You'll Go (to Change Your Name and Sex/Gender Marker)

Often, transgender and gender-nonbinary people face the challenge of going to court to change their name and sex/gender marker, and feel relieved when they're done. Prepare yourself for everything that comes after the magical moment your request is granted, though.

The name and sex you were assigned at birth will need to be changed in all kinds of places. The list below is not meant to be comprehensive, but gives you an idea of all the places you might have to update your information:

- airline programs
- bank accounts
- birth certificate
- cell phone provider
- College Board and ACT registrations
- college savings programs
- credit cards
- credit reporting bureaus
- drivers license
- gaming and other online accounts
- immunization records
- lost pet microchip databases
- medical records
- military and veterans affairs documentation
- online payment services accounts
- other licenses (FCC Radio Operator Licenses, industry certifications, etc.)
- religious ordination (holy orders in certain religions)
- school lunch account
- school records, transcripts, and diplomas
- scouting program registrations (Boy Scouts, Girl Scouts, etc.)
- Social Security or other social benefits registrations
- state education agency records
- utility accounts (electric, gas, water, etc.)
- voter registration
- wills (both your own and any wills you are mentioned in)

School-based Discrimination

It is possible that you will encounter discrimination for being transgender or gender-nonbinary at school, even if you've gone through the process of changing your name or your sex/gender marker. This might mean your school tries to prevent you from using the restroom or locker room that matches your gender identity, that teachers or staff are openly or subtly hostile to you, or that you are harassed by your peers and nothing is done about it. In these situations, you may be able to take legal action to address and end this discrimination against you. We go into more details on school-based discrimination later in this chapter.

Employment Discrimination

Employment discrimination is something transgender and gender-nonbinary people encounter on a regular basis. This might mean that you aren't hired for a job, that you are fired from your job, or that you are treated worse than your co-workers just because of your gender identity. While there should be laws protecting trans and nonbinary people from discrimination at work, there are currently no laws at the Federal level preventing it. Some states and several cities have laws that protect transgender and gender-nonbinary people at work, though, so make sure you research the laws in your area. There's a link to a map of state-by-state laws in the resources section. To find out if your city has discrimination protections, you should reach out to local LGBTQIA+ organizations or search your city's website.

Housing Discrimination

Finding and keeping housing is another area where transgender and gender-nonbinary people face discrimination on a regular basis. This might mean that someone refuses to rent an apartment to you, that they kick you out of your apartment, or they treat you worse than other tenants. Like employment discrimination, there are no laws at the Federal level preventing it, but some states and several cities have laws that protect transgender and gender-nonbinary people's right to fair housing.

Steps for Dealing With School-Based Discrimination

For transgender and gender-nonbinary youth, school is the most likely place they will experience discrimination. While each situation will be different, there are some common steps and things to keep in mind if you're going to fight back against mistreatment:

- Follow the procedure for reporting discrimination that is required by your school or school district. These are often not written or designed in a way that is friendly to the person reporting, but you have a stronger case by showing that you tried to follow the steps you were supposed to. It also keeps the school or school district from saying that they would have done something had you just followed their policy.

- If you have a Gender and Sexuality Alliance club at your school, reach out to them to see what help they can offer. These clubs are usually sponsored by a teacher or other staff member who is an advocate for LGBTQIA+ youth and may have an influence in the school to make things better.

- Document the who/what/when/where/why/how at every step of your fight. Having a detailed timeline of what happened and when and who you talked to will be really helpful in putting together a picture of the event and the impact it had.

- Keep *everything*. You never know what random piece of paper or quickly scribbled note about a phone call or conversation about your situation will come in handy. Don't worry about the format or organization of it; if your case ends up going to court, the organization or lawyers assisting you will put together the pieces.

- If you've tried to follow the process for reporting discrimination and nothing is done, or the outcome isn't what you expected, you can contact a legal non-profit organization specializing in helping with school-based discrimination. If they aren't able to take your case, you can also seek out a private lawyer.

- If you aren't shy, you can contact the media to see if they will run a story about your situation and draw attention to your fight. Media pressure can be effective and bring things to a quicker, more positive conclusion than pursuing legal action.

My own validity has been and continues to be a huge issue for me. How can my gender be real if people won't even acknowledge that it exists? This acknowledgement is incredibly important to me, so it always gives me a spark of joy when I'm taking an online quiz or filling out a questionnaire and there's an option to pick "other" in response to the gender question. From Buzzfeed quizzes to online surveys, from passports to driver's licenses, it would be incredibly validating to have other genders to be a standard option on these documents.

Though an F for female, M for male, or O for other on my birth certificate, driver's license, or passport seems tiny and insignificant, it would give me immense joy to know that my gender is real from a legal standpoint. Legal recognition of nonbinary people would be a huge step forward for the understanding of gender in society.

Creating official mechanisms and institutions that recognize nonbinary people would show me the government thinks I'm real and valid and, honestly, if the government can help me, anyone can.

E.

Healthcare Decisions If You Are a Minor

Healthcare decision-making power is a place transgender and gender-nonbinary youth encounter legal barriers. Unfortunately, if both your parents don't approve of you starting medical transition, there's not much a court can do. However, if one parent approves and the other doesn't, there are situations where the approving parent can seek permission from a court to make those medical decisions for you against the wishes of the other parent.

Immigration and Emigration

We live in a world that is not kind to immigrants, especially LGBTQIA+ immigrants. Because laws about immigration and treatment of immigrants change so rapidly, it's hard to say what challenges you might encounter if you are an immigrant who is also transgender or gender-nonbinary. There are, however, great organizations that are able to help. Check those out at the end of the chapter.

If you are looking to emigrate to another country, it's a good idea to research the laws and protections for transgender and gender-nonbinary people while you're making your decision. You can research these countries on the internet, and visit their embassy or consulates to talk with people who work for the government in those countries to learn more.

I'm at a point in my life where politics wear me out. The more I hear about trans rights being stripped away or challenged by numerous bills in numerous states, the more I want to sit in my bed looking at photos of cats and forgetting these situations exist. Yet I don't get that luxury anymore, as now I have to keep up to date with who's taking what right of mine away. Is it the president? My governor? It's like playing the lottery but with the deconstruction of trans rights. It makes me feel as if it's pointless, as if waking up every day and living the way I want to is a burden on other people, and I hate that I feel that way. For me to have to make myself feel awful to suit the comforts of other people is ridiculous. I don't care that a man in North Carolina, whom I've never met, feels unsafe at the vague concept regarding my existence; I shouldn't have to beat myself down and hide myself to suit his own unfounded fears. I am not dangerous, I am not a pedophile, I am not a criminal. I am a person, I deserve the right to life, liberty, and the pursuit of happiness, just like every person should have those rights. To say I am somehow undeserving of that is blatant transphobia, whether rooted in hate or ignorance. Trans people have always existed, have always been people, have always lived their lives throughout history. The only difference now is that we aren't going to allow people to erase us.

Luka

Professionals vs. Pro Se

Transition, no matter what kind you pursue, is expensive. And money is the absolute worst. It's no surprise that transgender and gender-nonbinary people, who are already at an economic and social disadvantage, would want to find ways to save money at each step of transition.

If you can afford to use a lawyer to help with your legal transition steps, you should. They have specific knowledge, expertise, and relationships that make it more likely that you get the outcome you're looking for when going to court. To find a lawyer who has experience working with trans and nonbinary people, reach out to non-profits in your area who work with LGBTQIA+ people. And even if they refer you to someone who doesn't feel comfortable taking your case, lawyers are often willing and able to refer you to someone they know.

You can also file and represent yourself in court. In the United States, this is called "filing pro se." Pro se is a Latin phrase that means "on one's own behalf" and describes a situation where a person (who is 18 or older, or their parents or guardians if they are under 18) goes to court without a lawyer to represent them and their interests. Depending on where you live in the world, this concept of representing yourself might go by a different name, or you may not be able to represent yourself at all. It's important to understand your options before taking any steps.

You Will Always Be You

The process of legal transition and confronting other legal issues can be really exhausting. It's okay to take breaks, ask for help, give up, and try again. The biggest benefit you have in all of this is that you already know who you are and no court, school, employer, or agency can take that away from you.

It may take one try or many tries to get your legal documentation to align with who you are, but you will always be you.

Kathryn

One of the best parts of my job working with LGBTQIA+ youth is accompanying them and their and families when they go to court for legal name and sex/gender marker changes.

Many of the families we help cannot afford legal representation, so they file their petitions pro se using forms that have been developed by the transgender and gender-nonbinary community here in Texas to make the process a little easier.

It's always scary for me when we go to court, but not for the reasons you might think. Yes, the courthouse is a dark, dingy, intimidating place. Yes, there are security people at the doors. And yes, some of the clerks are a little prickly. But the scariest part is knowing that our families are representing themselves without the safety net of having a lawyer in case something goes wrong.

Thankfully, our families are well-prepared when they go to court and we usually get the outcome we want. And still, I'm always reminded of just how lonely the process of transition can be, and so it's always an honor to walk with our families through that process and be there at the moment that they become legally recognized as the person they have always known themselves to be.

Additional Resources

For more conversations and thoughts about legal transition and issues, here are a few resources:

thetransbook.com/link/0901
National Center for Transgender Equality has an amazing resource on their website called the ID Documents Center. It can help you figure out how to get a legal name change and update your sex/gender marker on state and federal identification documents.

thetransbook.com/link/0902
The American Civil Liberties Union can help you in cases of legal discrimination. Their website is an amazing place to learn about legal issues facing LGBTQIA+ youth and provides resources for schools that are interested in implementing policies to protect and support transgender and gender-nonbinary youth.

thetransbook.com/link/0903
The Transgender Legal Defense and Education Fund fights to end discrimination and to achieve equality for transgender and gender-nonbinary people. You can apply for their Name Change Project to get matched with a pro bono (a Latin term for "free") legal help getting a name change.

thetransbook.com/link/0904
The Transgender Law Center has a great resources section for transgender and gender-nonbinary immigrants.

thetransbook.com/link/0905
The Human Rights Campaign's website has a helpful map that explains the various employment protections for LGBTQIA+ people in the United States.

thetransbook.com/link/0906
Lambda Legal, a 501(c)(3) nonprofit, is a national organization committed to achieving full recognition of the civil rights of lesbians, gay men, bisexuals, transgender people and everyone living with HIV through impact litigation, education, and public policy work.

RELATIONSHIPS

CHAPTER 10

DATING

Do you ever wonder where to find people to date, when to tell someone who you're interested in that you're trans, how to ask someone out, what flirting even is, how to deal with people fetishizing you for your identity/parts/body, and other dating and relationship related questions? That's what this chapter is here to help you with!

At some point, you may have specific questions about dating that aren't covered here because your individual relationships will always be unique. Hopefully, you'll be able to take the information from this chapter and apply it—and you can always get ideas and suggestions from friends and trusted adults.

Are You Into Someone? Are They Into you?

Knowing whether you're sexually and/or romantically into a person sometimes comes easily, but it's not always so clear. Some of the signs that you like someone are:

- feeling happy around them
- wanting to be around them more often
- wanting to make them laugh
- feeling butterflies in your stomach
- thinking about them all the time
- wondering whether they like you
- wanting to touch your genitals to their genitals

After you've figured out that you're interested in someone, the next step is to decide what (if anything) to do about it. There are some people who are great to pursue or to ask out—and some people who it may be better if you don't. A close friend, for example, could be a great person to date if everything goes well, but a close friend could also be a hard to date if it hurts the friendship.

Part of the question about whether to pursue someone has to do with whether they're interested in you. But how can you know? Often disappointingly, the only way to know for sure if someone is into you is if they tell you they are. As long as there have been people, they have wished for ways to find out if someone is interested in them without actually having to talk with them about it! And while it's true we can make guesses based on someone's body language, what kinds of things they say to you, how often they text, and other things, it's not an absolute science. People can accidentally give a message that they're into you when they're just being friendly. They may also be so into you that they become standoffish and awkward. So the only fool-proof way to know if someone is interested in you is to just ask.

That being said, you can ask in a beating-around-the-bush kind of way. For example, asking someone if they have a crush on anyone can start the conversation without tying it to you specifically. Flirting is the most common way to indicate an interest in someone. So knowing how to flirt, and being able to spot it when other people are flirting with you, is incredibly useful.

Karen

This chapter is all about dating people. But you don't have to date anyone. In fact, many people are happiest when they're not dating anyone, don't want to date anyone, and would say no if someone asked them out on a date. Almost all of the stories our culture tells through movies, songs, etc., are about dating - so if you don't want to date someone, it's easy to feel like you're "wrong." But you're not. Never feel pressured to date just for the sake of dating. The only time dating is any good at all is if you're really into it!

As a gay trans man, my dating options are rather limited. Pretty much anytime there's a gay or bi man in my general area, you can guarantee I'm probably going to have a crush on them. That may also be the polyamory part of me, but the point is that I can't exactly be picky when it comes to romance. I haven't dated anyone since my girlfriend from a few years ago, and no guy has had a crush on me in that period of time, or at least hasn't told me. It's very hard for me to get back into the dating scene, outside of casual flirting with dudes I come into contact with. If they aren't straight or outright bigoted, they're only into cis men or post-op trans men, which is an impossible standard for me to meet. I haven't attempted any online dating, since I'm not really privy to having a bunch of random people judging my appearance and then, inevitably, sending me a nude. So that leaves me in the rather romantically void position of wanting a relationship, but having maybe .1% of the local population available who would be willing to date me. It can be very lonely, very crushing, and it sometimes makes me feel as if nobody would ever want me, however untrue that may be.

Luka

Flirting 101

Flirting is a way to let someone know you are romantically and/or sexually interested in them. It can be fun, light-hearted, and lacking in any serious interest, or it can be intense and connecting. Flirting can be intended to lead somewhere or it can be just for its own sake.

Some people love flirting. For them, flirting might come so naturally, they may give off a message that they're flirting with people who they don't even intend to flirt with. If this is you, and if it bothers you, there are ways to roll it back so your expressions match your intentions a little more fully. You can start by paying attention to how and where you touch people and how much direct eye contact you make. These are all cues that you are flirting. Of course, if you're okay with people thinking that you're flirting with them, no need to change a thing!

Flirting can also make people feel nervous. For them, there can be a whole host of issues that stop them from being the first person to engage. They might worry they're coming on too strong, that the other person won't flirt back, that their intentions will be misconstrued, or maybe they just feel plain uncomfortable flirting. If you are one of the people for whom flirting does not come naturally, and you want to improve your flirting game, here are a few things you can try with someone you'd like to flirt with:

- Show genuine interest in who they are by asking them about themselves. Ask follow-up questions to the things they share with you.

- Stand just a little closer to them than you do most people.

- Hold eye contact with them for a little longer than you do most people.

- Briefly touch their hand.

- Say playful, funny things.

But most—and maybe hardest—of all:

- Be yourself.

Flirting is supposed to be fun, but it can be scary too. If flirting still feels really weird to you, or it's just too far from how you normally interact with people, don't push yourself too hard. It's okay to slow down and even stop entirely. You can always pick it up again—or maybe flirting just isn't your thing. And that's okay too.

The most important part of flirting is showing someone a little more about yourself and how you interact with others. Pretending to be someone you're not won't work.

Asking Someone Out

Asking someone out can be exciting! Some people go all-out (like with prom-posals), while others opt for such a mellow approach that it could be mistaken for hanging out without any sexual or romantic intentions. The best approach to take depends on the person you're asking out. This could also be an opportunity to show them that you know them well enough to guess how they would like to be approached.

Spend some time to figure out how the person you're interested in would appreciate being asked out: text message, in person, video chat, etc. Ask yourself how they are most likely to reach out to you, and try to reach out to them in that way.

You'll also need to plan the date. You could hang out at the park, get dinner together, play putt-putt golf or pick-up basketball, go to the beach or a museum, or any number of things. Be creative: if the activity is unique, fun, and something they are interested in, the person will know you planned the outing for them specifically.

Once you've planned the outing, you gotta just dive in. Get up your courage, and ask the question.

But What If They're Not Into You?

Most people are turned down multiple times in their lives. If the person you want to date doesn't like you in that way, it doesn't mean you should give up or that there isn't a right person out there for you.

But also, it sucks. It's a disappointing feeling, especially if this is the only person you've been interested in for a long time. Sometimes it feels more than disappointing. It can feel lonely, sad, and depressing; you may even feel like no one will ever be into you. Unrequited, or non-returned, attraction is one of the hardest things to work through—but you can work through it.

Having your heart broken when you are still in the wishing, dreaming, and imaging phase of a relationship, before it's really even gotten started, can feel like physical pain even though it is emotional. Having resources like friends and hobbies to take your attention away from your pain is very helpful in moving past it.

Remember though, if you really care about someone, listen to what they tell you. If they tell you they aren't interested in you, figure out a way to either stop expressing your interest in them or, if you aren't able to do that, to stop talking with them entirely. For example, if you ask someone out, and they tell you they just want to be friends, you might see this as a hurtful response. Some people may call this being "friend-zoned." But friendship is important—more important for many people than a sexual or romantic relationship. While it's normal and okay to feel hurt, if you find yourself negatively expressing your anger or resentment or trying to change their minds, things have become problematic and you need to reconsider how you are interacting with them. If you love them, you will be respectful of them and their boundaries. If you aren't able to be happy as this person's friend, you can let them know and end the friendship.

Doing the Online Thing

There are so many ways to meet someone, each with their own benefits. When you meet someone in real life (IRL), there are certain pieces of known information. For example, if you meet someone through a mutual friend, there is someone to vouch for them. When you meet someone through an extracurricular activity, you know that you have something in common.

When you meet someone online, you can get to know their thoughts and feelings without the nervousness that usually comes with meeting them in person. You can also meet a much wider range of people online than you have access to in your daily life. But meeting someone online comes with a unique set of issues you need to account for as you get to know that person better. These issues apply to all of the digital ways you can meet people, including on dating sites, social media (particularly if you don't share any mutual IRL friends with the person), and people you meet online through friends.

Issues arise because it is easier to lie about who you are online. This is not to suggest that people don't lie IRL—because of course they do. And this is not to suggest that all people online lie—because of course most of them don't. But for those who do lie about important aspects of themselves online, meeting them IRL can be dangerous, which is why you need to set up extra safety measures. Here are a few tips on meeting someone IRL who you've met online:

- Meet in a public place. This deters people who are obviously not who they say they are.

- Bring someone else with you to the first meeting. They can sit with you or not, but be sure the person who you are meeting meets them too. This is about safety in numbers, but it's also about someone having your back if they get creepy vibes.

- Don't rush things. It's easy to feel emotionally close to someone you've talked with for hours and hours over days, weeks, or even months online. But when you meet them IRL, you're removing a certain protection. Sure, a person you're in an online relationship with can hurt you emotionally, but if you meet them IRL, they can also hurt you physically. Meeting someone you met online IRL is good because it means opening yourself up to a different kind of love, connection, and relationship, but be aware and protect yourself by being careful and thoughtful.

When you have a deep emotional connection to someone online, it can be hard to remember these guidelines. Maybe they live far away and don't have a lot of time or flexibility when they come to meet you. Maybe they invited you to visit them, but you don't have money for a hotel. Maybe they have a pretty big social media presence, and you feel certain they're exactly who they say they are. But these protective guidelines don't actually require all that much—and if someone is pushing back hard against them, that's a red flag that they don't have your best interests at heart. Someone who is being honest about who they are and who really cares about you will want you to have all the safety measures in place so you will feel and be safe.

As long as safety is your priority, online relationships can be wonderful, fulfilling, and supportive. The internet can offer a community and connections you don't have access to IRL. It can provide resources, information, and support for you and your identity. Just make sure you enjoy everything awesome about the internet without putting yourself at any additional risk.

Disclosure

Telling the person you're dating about your gender identity could be tricky or it could be easy, depending on a number of factors.

If you are just coming out to yourself and the people around you, you might think of this as a part of the coming out process. Chapter 3 is probably the right place for you to be. Chapter 3 could also be helpful if you have recently come to fully understand your gender identity and are just starting to date someone.

If you are already living as your true self, how and when to disclose that information to your partner is somewhat different. If you are open with most people about being a trans or nonbinary person, you can include that easily in your conversations as you are getting to know someone.

However, many trans people who are not usually open about being trans struggle with knowing when and how to disclose that information to someone they are dating (or want to date). Disclosure in this situation is important because your transness is an important part of who you are, and a major part of the dating process is getting to know each other. Balance getting to know someone a little bit (and letting them get to know you a little bit), making sure you will be safe during the disclosing process, and telling them before they feel misled.

You may want to get to know each other before you disclose your full gender identity because you want to start off the process on a more open field. Your gender is an important part of who you are—but if it is not something that you typically talk about with strangers or acquaintances, it shouldn't come first in a dating relationship either.

By getting to know someone, you get a deeper glimpse into whether they are someone who you will feel safe disclosing your identity to. You can have casual conversations about genders and identities and expectations along with other casual conversations about whether you like to cook, you're into anime, and what your favorite color is. Once you feel safe with sharing deeper, more private parts of who you are, that is the time to start thinking about sharing your gender identity.

However, you need to talk about your gender identity before you become deeply emotionally intimate or engage in sexual activities with someone. Personal connections of those sorts require that both people trust each other and the information they know about each other. The fullness of your gender identity should be part of that equation.

Disclosing can be scary. What if they reject you because you're trans? Well, then they aren't the right person for you to be in a relationship with. In fact, they've done you a favor by showing you who they really are without you needing to take up any more time and energy. Just as if they'd rejected you for one of many other reasons—maybe you're a vegetarian and they can't imagine dating someone who doesn't eat meat. Or maybe you know you'll never, ever want to parent children and they're quite certain that they do. You'll notice that none of these things (no meat/meat, no children/children) are inherently good or bad or right or wrong—it's more about the match of the two of you. And the same thing is true of someone who doesn't want to date you because you are trans. They aren't the right person for you.

Kathryn

Disclosure was the hardest part of transition for me. It felt scary to think about meeting someone for a date and then disclosing my trans identity to them at some point. Would I be safe? How would they react? How would I handle rejection in public?

At some point, I'm not exactly sure when, I started disclosing first thing—whether in my profile on dating apps, or working it into conversation when meeting someone in person. Not only did this make me feel safer (because there was no build-up of anxiety before disclosure—it was out of the way in the beginning), it made me more confident. Being able to own and embrace my trans identity as an asset made me more attractive to potential partners, even those who hadn't dated a trans person before.

Fetishizing

There are many people who find trans and nonbinary people more attractive than people with other gender identities. Which is great! It means that there are people who will know you are the best person for them to be with, not in spite of who you are, but particularly because of who you are.

There are also people who are attracted to trans and nonbinary people because of who they are . . . but in a way that feels creepy or uncomfortable. They may be interested in a person who is trans or nonbinary because they have a fetish—or a particularly strong sexual interest or obsession—in a trans or nonbinary person's body, rather than because of the multilayered, complex, beautiful person they are. Dating websites targeting trans and nonbinary people (like MyTransgenderCupid.com) are often created for this kind of person, which means they are often not the best places for people who are trans and nonbinary to find healthy relationships. Unfortunately, when there isn't any other option out there for meeting people, sometimes these sites are the only options available.

Being fetishized, or being the recipient of a person's fetish interest, can sometimes feel strong and empowering ("Wow! Someone is really, really into me!"), can sometimes feel overwhelming ("Ugh! This is way too much attention on my body. They should pay attention to me, to who I am!"), and can sometimes feel confusing ("I wish I knew how I felt about this. Sometimes it's good, sometimes it's gross."). Sometimes you may not care one way or the other. If someone is fetishizing you, it is more about who they are, not about you, your body, or who you are. Regardless of your feelings or reactions to someone being interested in you as a fetish, it's important to know what's going on, because that helps to inform how you choose to react.

People who are interested in a trans or nonbinary person as an object of their fetish are usually just interested in sex. They may even feel they have a "right" to have sex with a trans or nonbinary person, or that the person should feel "grateful" someone wants to have sex with them. These are examples of how attention from someone with a fetish can feel gross because they are wrong. They do not have a right to any kind of attention from you, physical or emotional, and you should never think you have to feel grateful that someone wants to have sex with you. You are a full and worthy person who has the capacity to build a beautiful, mutually fulfilling sexual relationship.

Figuring out whether someone is interested in you as a whole person or is only interested in your body as a fetish can be hard—particularly because some people who have fetishes have learned how to cover up their fetish to increase the likelihood that a trans or nonbinary person will connect and be sexual with them. This is why building a relationship with someone before being sexual with them is an important safety measure, for both your physical and emotional safety.

Breaking Up

The end of a relationship can be painful and sad, regardless of whether you are the one ending it or not. This is partly because of social expectations about relationships that end (that a relationship is a "failure" if it ends before someone dies), and the hopes and dreams that often accompany a relationship (often about the future trajectory of the relationship, including the end of the daily interactions).

Deciding to end a relationship is the first step. You may be ending it because of a change in your or the other person's life (like one of you graduated and/or is moving away), because you've met someone you would rather be in a relationship with, because what you want in a relationship has changed, or a whole host of other reasons. As you are figuring this out, it's important to know what you want and don't want, to clearly communicate that to the other person, and to not take too long in going through with the conversation.

When you think you want to break up with someone, but you hesitate because you're worried about how they will take it or whether you'll find someone else, you are actually hurting them more. Dragging out a dead or dying relationship is not good for you or the other person, even if they try to convince you otherwise. They need time to move on and heal, and that can't happen while they're still in a relationship with you.

If you are the one ending the relationship, consider the other person's feelings in the process. Be clear that you are ending the relationship, tell them why if you feel comfortable doing so, and then be the one to draw boundaries. You cannot support them emotionally while they heal; they need to lean on their other support networks. If they don't have any other support networks, you might connect them with therapists or other services at school or through other community resources. They won't be able to heal while maintaining the same depth of connection with you.

Most of my straight friends seem to have a new crush every day and a new boo every week. Call me crazy, but I'm jealous! As a black, queer, nonbinary individual, I have a lot of boxes that need to be checked before I become interested in a person. Not racist? Check. Not homophobic? Check. Not transphobic? Check. Will respect my pronouns? Check. Most of the time, though, a couple of those boxes are left blank.

My struggles with finding people I would even want to date parallel the difficulties I have finding kinship with the communities of which I am a part. I share a cultural experience with black people, but homophobia is rampant in the black community. I share a sexual experience with queer people, but the LGBTQ+ community leaves little room for cultural icons aside from those predominantly white symbols of gay culture. I share a gender-related experience with trans people, but the trans community often fails to include those of us who require something other than a male-female dichotomy.

I want whoever I date to be someone I'm comfortable with, someone who I feel doesn't judge any part of me. It's hard to find that someone, especially in high school, when we're all just trying to understand how the world works and how to live in our own skins. Hopefully, as the people with whom I will interact grow and mature, dating will become easier—but for now, I think I'll stay alone until I find someone who checks all my boxes.

E.

If you are not the one ending the relationship, the experience is usually even more emotionally difficult, particularly if you are not expecting it. It can even be hard to accept what's happening. Nevertheless, you have to accept it. Hopefully, the relationship was able to bring you joy, love, and learning during the time that it existed. But when someone breaks up with you, it's time to let the relationship be part of your past. That doesn't mean it is any less important to who you are or who you will become.

Regardless of who has ended a relationship, filling what can feel like a void is difficult for most people—emotionally, physically, and even socially, during your day. Fill the void with friends, hobbies, family, games, and working out (anything you enjoy) is a critical part of doing what must be done: moving on.

But Most of All, It Should Be Fun

If you're not having fun dating, take a hard look at the situation. Dating is supposed to give you and your partner a fun, emotionally fulfilling connection. So play video games, take long walks, bake extravagant cakes, watch movies, play card games, dance, go bowling, and do all of the other things that bring you both joy together! That's where the really good parts of dating happen.

An Important Note on Safety

If you are ending a relationship because you do not feel physically or emotionally safe, then the other person's feelings don't matter. End the relationship from a distance (like by text, email, voicemail, etc.) and surround yourself with people who you trust who know about the situation. They will help you maintain your safety. More information about unsafe relationships is in Chapter 11 and Chapter 12.

Additional Resources

For more conversations and thoughts about dating (trans-specific and general), here are a few resources:

thetransbook.com/link/1001
Captain Awkward offers long, specific, and thoughtful responses to young people's questions about love and relationships.

thetransbook.com/link/1002
This video outlines the science behind heartbreak, explaining how sadness about a broken heart can impact a person. It's useful to know how your body might react to the end of a relationship.

thetransbook.com/link/1003
This short essay, written by a trans woman, discusses the ways that safety plays into all of her decisions about dating.

CHAPTER II

HEALTHY V. UNHEALTHY RELATIONSHIPS, CONSENT, SAFETY, AND OTHER RELATIONSHIP BUZZWORDS

There are so many different things people say are musts in sexual and romantic relationships: relationship health, trust, consent, safety, and more. They've become buzzwords that are thrown around a lot, sometimes with definitions and context and sometimes without. This chapter will break down what each of these ideas really means, why they're important, how to figure out what you really want, communicating what you want to another person, and listening to what they want. It also talks about listening to what your friends have to say about your relationships—because while your friends' perceptions aren't always easy to hear, they are often important to at least consider.

Healthy v. Unhealthy Relationships

Determining whether a relationship is healthy or not can be easy (clearly, a relationship where someone is being physically hurt by their partner is unhealthy), but sometimes it's not. Understanding the ways that relationships work to provide health and support for each partner instead of pain and a lack of health involves a thoughtful understanding of a number of relationship dynamics: Respect, Equality, Safety, and Trust. These four elements, according to the Columns and Shadows: A Healthy Relationship Model, are explained in the sections below.

Respect

Respect is "a feeling or understanding that someone or something is important, serious, etc., and should be treated in an appropriate way."

Respect is about appreciating your partner's viewpoints, opinions, beliefs, and decisions—both in general, and regarding your relationship. It's about setting and observing boundaries, asking your partner for their input and hearing them when they say "Yes," "No," or "Maybe."

And respect is about recognizing the importance of the relationship you're in. Following the guidelines you've set up for each other, treating the relationship with care, or at least the amount and type of care that you know your partner expects.

Equality

In this context, we're talking about the equality of "being equal, especially in status, rights, and opportunities." Take special note here that we're using the word equality (instead of the social-justice-context "equity") intentionally. We aren't looking for fair amounts of access, but a truly balanced amount of power among the people in the relationship.

Equality is about making decisions together, or at least creating agreements for how decisions will be made. It's about both partners having the same amount of voice and power, and knowing that the partners in a relationship have an open seat at the decision-making table (even if they don't choose to sit in it).

This can be tough, because everyone is navigating the very unequal world-at-large with different amounts of power (some of us granted more, others less, because of our social identities), so it's easy for us to either recreate those dynamics in our relationships, or invert them to a different, but still harmful, outcome.

Safety

Safety is "the condition of being protected from or unlikely to cause danger, risk, or injury" with one big caveat: at the cause or negligence of your partner. That is, a healthy relationship doesn't require safety from the weather, poverty, or an errant banana peel. It's safety with and from each other in the relationship.

Safety is about knowing that your partner won't intentionally hurt you—physically, emotionally, psychologically, sexually, or otherwise. It's knowing that they are looking out for you, for your interests, and for your general well-being.

You're not going to be able to protect each other from everything, but if you are having a hard time, you know they'll be there to support you.

Trust

Trust is "the belief that someone or something is reliable, good, honest." A mutual trust that the partners in the relationship can believe one another, rely on one another, and be generally good to one another.

Trust is knowing that you can believe your partner, that they are saying what they mean, and that when they act you can reasonably assume they're acting in ways that are good. It's knowing that you aren't being manipulated, mislead, or taken advantage of.

Columns and Shadows

The way these four elements impact relationships are either by being a column or a shadow. An element of a relationship is a column if it is presented without condition, exception, or pressure, and you can respond or act in a way that you are comfortable with. These are good things that help to hold a relationship up and to keep it strong and healthy. An element of a relationship is a shadow if it is presented with conditions, exceptions, or pressure, and it requires you to act or respond in a way you are uncomfortable with. These are things that may look like columns because they are shadows or have the same shape of them, but they are not sturdy.

Thinking about the ways that parts of your relationships are columns and parts are shadows can help you to understand and consider whether your relationship is more healthy or more unhealthy. Because unhealthy relationships are not always easy to spot, this way of thinking can help you see your relationship dynamics with more clarity. Here is a picture of the model:

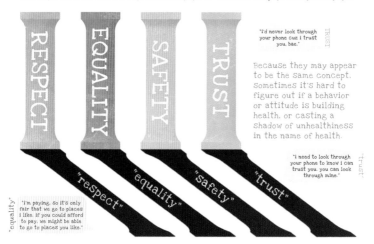

COLUMNS & SHADOWS: A Healthy Relationship Model

A Healthy Relationship is Shaped by RESPECT, EQUALITY, SAFETY, & TRUST

Behaviors & attitudes that fall into one of these categories can appear in one of two ways: as columns (sturdy, reliable, yay!) or shadows (empty, shifty, not yay.).

RESPECT EQUALITY SAFETY TRUST

"I'd never look through your phone cuz I trust you, bae."

Because they may appear to be the same concept, sometimes it's hard to figure out if a behavior or attitude is building health, or casting a shadow of unhealthiness in the name of health.

"I need to look through your phone to know I can trust you. you can look through mine."

"respect" "equality" "safety" "trust"

"equality" "I'm paying, so it's only fair that we go to places I like. if you could afford to pay, we might be able to go to places you like."

HOW TO KNOW?! Well, A Behavior or Attitude is PROBABLY...

a HEALTHY COLUMN of R.E.S.T. if

☺ it's presented without condition, exception, or pressure, and

☺ you can respond or act in a way you are comfortable with.

an UNHEALTHY SHADOW of R.E.S.T. if

☹ it's only presented with conditions, exceptions, or pressure, and

☹ it requires you to act or respond in a way you are uncomfortable with.

www.unhushed.org
Reprinted with permission.

The language in this model is not common, so if you want to use it as a way to talk with a friend or a partner, you'll probably have to show them this picture and talk with them about what it means.

Most of what I learned about consent, I learned from Tumblr. And that's ...a problem. Don't get me wrong, Tumblr is cool, but it's not the most reliable source for critical sex education information. Honestly, though, had it not been for some really passive aggressive textposts, I would know nothing, and that's super unfortunate.

Questionable though it may be, I actually found Tumblr to be a really helpful resource. I learned that you should get consent before any kind of physical contact, whether it be a hug, a kiss, or sexual activity. I wish I had known I could say no to anything, and I wish more people knew and cared about consent, in both sexual and non-sexual scenarios. Sometimes, I don't feel like giving anyone a hug—interactions with an expectation of physical contact would be so much easier if people asked first.

As I've learned more, I've realized how little other people know about consent. Even people who try to respect their partners don't necessarily realize that they should ask before kissing someone. This worries me somewhat; if people who are trying to be kind and respectful don't fully understand consent, how can we expect those who may be less conscientious to do so?

E.

Consent

Consent, at its most basic level, means to tell someone whether you agree to something or not. But usually when people talk about consent, they're talking about whether someone has said yes to sexual activity. From there, consent just gets more and more complicated. Because there has been so much attention on consent in the past few years, especially at the college level, it's worth looking at the language people have used to discuss it.

Karen

Consent is so complex. The ideas behind consent can even be complicated to talk about—and it gets so much more difficult to understand exactly what's happening when you are actually with someone who you care about. Don't let difficulty stop you from having the conversations! It's okay to have conversations where you disagree with your partner and talk about your feelings and ask about their feelings.

No Means No

When consent first became a word people were thinking and talking a lot about, the understanding that when someone said that they did not want to engage in sexual behavior ("No means no!"), they actually meant it and that they should stop being asked/pressured into sexual behavior, it was a pretty big deal. Before that, many people (especially men) had been taught that many other people (especially women) didn't really mean no. Instead, they were trying to say they weren't "easy" and if they were just asked enough and/or in the right way, they would give in. That was a recipe for sexual assault and rape. It made a huge difference. But it also left out plenty of potential scenarios—like when a person says no through body language, when they are asleep or unconscious, when they are unsure of what they want, when they are too drunk or otherwise incapable of expressing their opinion, to name a few examples.

Yes Means Yes

When people realized that believing people when they said no to sex wasn't enough to really be consensual, they moved along to the idea that to have consent, everyone had to enthusiastically say "Yes!" This was great, for a while. But it got taken a little too far—with people thinking that unless there was explicit, verbal consent to every sexual activity, it was nonconsensual. This was ultimately seen as too rigid a way to understand sexual consent. For example, it left people who were in longer term relationships in an awkward place where they were required to talk about each activity rather than build a relationship that had a deeper context of mutuality.

The ways people have moved on to talk about consent are varied. Here are a few of the (many) different ideas about what consent is:

Tea Consent is a blog post turned into a YouTube video from a few years ago that, more or less, says if you wouldn't force someone to drink tea, why would you force them to have sex? It points out that if someone is asleep or unconscious, they want neither tea nor sex. It also points out that just because someone wanted tea last week, they can still turn down tea this week. Same thing for sex—just because they wanted it before, doesn't mean they want it now. This is, in some ways, a fancy way of repeating that no means no.

FRIES comes from Planned Parenthood. It's pretty comprehensive. FRIES includes both no-means-no and yes-means-yes, along with some other ideas that are useful, like saying consent is only about specific activities rather than "sex" generally. Also, who doesn't love fries?

From "Sexual Consent" by Planned Parenthood, Copyright 2019 by author. Reprinted with permission.

Consent Castle says consent is like a building a castle. When you start building a castle with someone, you have to talk about your plans. You have to talk about what you want and don't want in a castle. You have to be specific. These are all analogies for talking to someone about what kind of touch (and, maybe eventually, what kind of sex) they like and want from your relationship.

Once you actually start building the castle (i.e., having sex), you have to wear hard hats and use safety gear (like condoms). You have to check in with your castle buddy about whether they like the direction you're going in and you have to change course if they don't.

After your castle is built, everyone can get pretty comfortable. You don't talk about the details of it as much, although you may decide to change things up by painting or even building on a new room. This part of the analogy is talking about a long-term relationship, where you may have decided you aren't going to wear condoms anymore. But if you decide to have sex in a different kind of way, you'll need to go back to talking about things before you get started.

This idea of consent is much more complicated than the other two. But that's not necessarily a bad thing, because consent is more complicated than a lot of people realize.

Consent in relationships involving trans people is so, excruciatingly crucial. Already, in my own experience, trans people have difficulty finding partners, and much less healthy partners who will listen and take care of them. I know that often times, as a gay trans man, I wonder if maybe I could just date a straight man, or a lesbian. I'm what they want physically, why shouldn't I? But the reality is that a relationship would likely end with them either not respecting my gender or with me simply living in that relationship as woman. Both scenarios end up with a bad outcome for both parties. And then when you try to add sex into that mix? Sex with a trans person has to include a talk about boundaries—it just has to. There's literally no way to avoid that for everyone involved to have a safe and fun time.

Luka

So Which One Is Best?

Well, they're all useful. The thing about consent is that it's not simple and easy. It's something we have to pay attention to, think about, talk about, and make part of our sexual relationships. Without consent, a relationship cannot be healthy. Each of these ideas can be thought of as scoops of ice cream in a banana split. They all have their place—and together they make up a fantastic dessert.

Love

Is love a relationship buzzword? We're going to go with yes, because it's rarely defined and it's popular to say!

There are many different theories and definitions of love. Here are a few of them:

- **Love Languages:** People show love differently. Some people show love by giving gifts, spending quality time together, saying kind words, doing things for the other person, and/or physically touching the other person. (The Five Love Languages: How to Express Heartfelt Commitment to Your Mate is a 1995 book by Gary Chapman).

- **Three Loves Theory:** There are three kinds of romantic/sexual love: lust, passion, and commitment. They do not depend or necessarily build on one another, they all happen on their own time, and they have unique elements. Lust is immediate and short lived. Passion arises out of knowing a person, but usually wears off after you know someone very well. Commitment is the one that can make a relationship last.

- **Triangle Theory of Love:** Love is made up of three elements: intimacy, passion, and commitment. How much of each element is present in a relationship defines the kind of relationship it is. For example, infatuation is just passion while romantic love is passion and intimacy combined. (http://www.robertjsternberg.com/love/)

Clearly, love is anything but clear. Nevertheless, we're always trying to understand it because it plays such a huge role in our lives and relationships.

Here are a few interesting things to know about love:

- Many languages have more than one word for different kinds of love, like love a parent has for a child, love that is mostly sexual, love that is new and emerging, and love that has been felt for a long, long time.
- When we love someone, our brains have unique, physiological reactions to both being near them and being separate from them.
- Falling in love can have similar physiological effects as addiction. Losing love, or having a broken heart, causes the pain centers of the brain to light up, which means we are feeling physical pain.

All of which is to say, love is pretty great when you're feeling it and pretty horrible when you're missing it. But you don't have to run away with those feelings—either end of them. If you keep your head about you, you'll be better able to make decisions that are the best for you in both the short term and the long term.

Boyfriend, Girlfriend, Partner, Lover . . .

What's the right word to use anyway? On the next page is a list of words that could describe someone you are in a romantic and/or sexual relationship with. You'll probably like some of these words and not like others at all—the same goes for the person you're dating. It's important to make sure that you only use descriptions that the person you're describing actually likes—especially if you are dating someone who is nonbinary, because a lot of these words are gender specific.

BEAU

LOVER

MY HUMAN

PARTNER

You might choose one, none, or all! Just be sure that the person you're talking about likes the name(s) you're calling them.

Baby Love	Love Muffin	My Human
Babycake	Lover	My Love
Beau	Main Squeeze	My Lover
Boo	Media Naranja	My Main Squeeze
Boo Thang	Mi Rey/Reyna/	My One
Boy Toy	Reyne	My Other Half
Boyfriend	My \<name\>	My Person
Captain Boyfriend	My Baby	My Sweet One
Companion	My Beau	My Sweetie
Date	My Beloved	Paramour
Datefriend	My Better Half	Partner
Doctor Girlfriend	My Boyf/Girlf	Partner in Crime
Escort	My Cutie	Partner Person
Friend	My Datefriend	Person I am dating
Frisky Friend	My Dude	Significant Other
Gentleman Caller	My Fellow	(SO)
Girlfriend	My Gal	Soul Mate
Heart	My Goofball	Suitor
Hoss	My Guy	Sweetheart
Love Collaborator	My Hot Stuff	Twin Flame

What Does This Have to Do With Being Trans?

The short and easy answer is that this is all the same for trans, cis, nonbinary people, everyone. Relationships are healthy or unhealthy regardless of the gender identities of the people involved.

The more nuanced and complex answer is that trans and nonbinary people are statistically more likely to be abused by a partner, so they are less likely to be in a healthy relationship. (See Chapter 12 for more details.) But statistics are most important when it comes to conversations about whole populations—not as much about you or your specific relationships. So as with everything, take what is useful, leave what is not.

Additional Resources

thetransbook.com/link/1101
Scarleteen is the best one-stop-shop for information about relationships, sex, and sexuality online. They have been around since 1998 and offer moderated discussion boards so the trolls don't take over.

thetransbook.com/link/1102
To learn more about the Columns and Shadows healthy relationships model, check out this blog post.

thetransbook.com/link/1103
This Tea Consent video teaches consent in a very approachable and very British way.

thetransbook.com/link/1104
This website explains the Three Loves Theory in more detail.

CHAPTER 12

RELATIONSHIP AND SEXUAL VIOLENCE

iolence is harmful whether it is emotional, sexual, or physical. This chapter is about those kinds of violence. Even relationships that are supposed to be safe havens from violence and unwelcoming, scary parts of the world can turn toxic, risky, and damaging. The scary fact is that trans people are at a higher risk for intimate partner violence than almost anyone else. This chapter is about warning signs, ways to find support, and other potentially life-saving information about supporting yourself and your trans community through the hardest parts of relationships.

Things We Shouldn't Have to Say

You should never be pressured into anything you are uncomfortable with. Ever. Period.

We hope for a world where everyone knows they are the true authorities over their own bodies. We dream of a future where personal autonomy wins every time. Where no one is ever pressured to say yes. Where relationships bloom out of a mutual love and respect and end under the same circumstances. This is not the world we live in.

You are worthy of this world we dream of. If anyone ever tells you otherwise, question everything about them and your relationship with them. They do not value you living your best life, and that's not okay.

Types of Violence

Violence in relationships is usually called intimate partner violence (or IPV). Other words for it include dating violence, dating abuse, relationship abuse, relationship violence, domestic abuse, and domestic violence. We'll mostly use the term IPV.

IPV can take many forms, and that's where a lot of problems happen. Because many people see IPV as meaning one thing (usually one person hitting their partner until they bleed or bruise), it's much harder to see the ways that IPV actually happens. Here are five types, as described in UN|HUSHED's (a sex education non-profit) sex education curricula:

- **Emotional and verbal:** When someone threatens, insults, or otherwise psychologically harms their partner or their date.
- **Financial:** When someone controls their partner's access to their own money.
- **Physical:** When someone hurts their partner's or their date's body.
- **Reproductive:** When someone controls their partner's reproduction by withholding contraception or forcing a pregnancy termination.
- **Sexual:** When someone forces or pressures their partner or their date into sexual contact they don't want.
- **Stalking:** When someone follows another person or repeatedly contacts them against their permission or will, causing fear.

The details of what each of these kinds of IPV looks like can vary.

Emotional and verbal violence can include telling a partner that they aren't good enough, outing them, or giving them backhanded compliments. An example of this might be, "You're really pretty for a trans girl." It sounds like a compliment ("pretty"), but it comes with a slam ("for a trans girl"). This specific kind of emotional violence is called negging.

Financial violence can mean that someone forces their partner to give them money, gifts, or to pay their bills. It could also be someone not letting their partner work to earn their own money by keeping them from going to a job interview, constantly nagging them to quit their job, or interfering with their work or school so they're fired or drop out.

Physical violence is the form of IPV that most people think of first, with examples like hitting, slapping, punching, or even choking. But there are other forms of physical violence, like pushing their partner out of their way or holding their partner's hand so tightly they can't pull it back.

Reproductive violence is a form of IPV where a person controls their partner's body by making choices about how and when they are pregnant or not pregnant. Some examples of sexual violence include forced kissing and snuggling or forced oral or penetrative intercourse. Stalking can include checking a partner's cell phone, emails, social networks, and messaging as well as physically following them, asking their friends where they are and why, and other ways of constantly paying attention to their physical whereabouts and who they are with.

Importantly, none of these forms of violence begin with the more invasive, more harmful forms of IPV. Instead, the violent partner starts off with lower level ways to encroach on their partner's sense of what is acceptable or not acceptable while they become increasingly reliant on one another. When the relationship has grown to a place of deep connection, the violent partner is able to slowly build to increasing levels of violence. Because this is the typical evolution of IPV, it is critical to be aware of warning signs that a relationship may be moving toward violence.

Warning Signs

These are the signals that a relationship is moving toward violence. They are often not recognized as violence in themselves, and they are not always the beginning steps of violence, but they are critical to be aware of.

- **Falsely accusing.** As is the case with many of these warning signs, being irrationally accused of things can hurt a person's feelings, make them sad, and leave them wanting to explain things to their partner. But this puts them in a place of apologizing and trying to make things right when they haven't done anything to warrant that.

- **Apologizing frequently.** If a partner is apologizing frequently, it's probably because they are doing something that requires frequent apologies. This is a warning sign. It is possible, of course, that they feel badly about themselves for no reason and are apologizing irrationally, but this is also a problem.

- **Being very jealous or insecure and requiring a lot of reassurance.** Jealousy and insecurity require a lot of reassurance. While it is natural for people to be occasionally jealous or insecure in a relationship, if those feelings are used as a way of restricting what the other person is doing, that is a step toward IPV.

- **Getting very angry.** Emotions are very hard to control in many instances; they're something that happens without us realizing until we're deep in them. But if a person gets angry quickly and frequently, that hurts the people around them and they need to learn how to manage their internal response systems. Anger can also be used as a way to manipulate others by (as with inappropriately accusing someone) making them feel badly about themselves.

- **Getting very close very quickly.** This can feel fun, exciting, passionate, and connecting, but when people get very close very quickly, they can miss learning important things about each other. It is also a technique used by people who are moving a relationship toward IPV because their partner then has a harder time breaking up with them, even though they've only been together for a short time.

- **Isolating from friends and/or family.** This can include saying things that make a person question how close they are to their friends and family, how much their friends and family love them, and whether their friends and family have their best interests at heart. While this isn't always the case for everyone's family or friends, that is something for them to determine, not for someone they're dating to decide or try to convince them of.

- **Judging clothes, especially by saying they're too revealing or sexy.** While this may be stated as a preference or even as concern for a partner's safety, it ultimately is about controlling someone, their choices, and their body. There is never a reason someone should try to change or control what their partner wears.

- **Pressure to do anything, including sexual activities, self-disclosure, drugs or alcohol, or going somewhere that makes a person uncomfortable.** This is just flat out wrong and a behavior that usually escalates. If someone pressures their partner to eat something they don't like or other low-stakes activities, that can easily turn into pressuring them to be sexual in a way they don't want over time.

- **Treating a partner differently when they're alone together versus when they're with friends (or when someone is not ever willing to introduce their partner to their friends).** This shows that a person regularly has two different personalities and that they don't want to show their friends who they really are with their partner. It's a form of disrespect.

Even if these warning signs don't indicate a potential for IPV, they are signs that the person has issues they need to work on before they are in a relationship. They need to find professional support, over and above what a partner might be able to offer them. If you find that someone you are dating is exhibiting these kinds of warning signs, but you don't feel like their behavior has escalated to IPV, have a talk with them. Tell them what they're doing is not okay and that it's a precursor to violence. Tell them you think they need to figure themselves and their relationship patterns out. Tell them you think you need to break off the relationship while they do that, and you're open to getting back together with them after they've done that work. These kinds of behaviors are not okay, and it's okay to stand up for yourself and make clear that you deserve to be treated better—because you do.

What to Do

Recognizing that something is not as it should be in a relationship, that it either has violent elements or warning signs leading to violence, is merely the first step. And it's not an easy step. The next steps involve making changes in the relationship, which is definitely harder.

If It's You Causing IPV

It is rare that we talk about what someone should do if they realize they are abusing their partner in one of the ways outlined above. But we need to. It is not always easy or clear what steps to take if you realize you are an abuser. It may be that the habits are so deeply ingrained, you didn't realize it until reading a description of your behavior in a book like this. It may be that these are relationship patterns you have seen with your parents, older siblings, in romantic movies, and other places that have led you to see them as normal. Congratulations on realizing that they are not normal!

The next step is changing your behavior. It's not possible for most people to just stop doing something; you have to replace what you've been doing with a different approach.

Kathryn

One of the most lonely times of my life was when I was experiencing IPV. The thing is, I didn't know that's what was happening. Because I wasn't being physically abused, I didn't think it counted as abuse. I thought I could help make my partner better, but that was part of the danger: in order to change them, I had to change myself and, at a certain point, I didn't recognize myself anymore. I hope my telling you that I've experienced IPV and got out and have gone on to have many loving, healthy relationships, helps you know you're not alone if you're in a toxic relationship right now, or find yourself in one in the future.

If It's You Experiencing IPV

If your partner is being violent toward you or exhibiting any of the warning signs leading to violence, move toward emotional and physical safety. Leaving an abusive relationship carries increased risks, so begin by building up your network of support. This is often the first thing to go when a relationship is becoming violent because it is incredibly hard to leave a relationship when you don't have a support network of friends or family. The abuser has set this dynamic up intentionally.

I have personally never dealt with relationship violence. I am the sort of person who cuts people out quickly if I think they may be toxic toward me. My family has made me realize that relationship violence is not limited to a significant other, as it may be found in any relationship. For example, how my grandparents would use a stick to whip my mother's legs. But the most prominent example of what abuse looks like in my life is how an uncle of mine would beat his much older girlfriend. Even somebody like me, who doesn't tolerate disrespect, couldn't see through him at first, until I actually saw what he was capable of.

That's what's most dangerous about these abusers, they know what they can and can't do in front of certain people. As a child, I was close to him. He would take care of me so well that even when I did something out of line he wouldn't yell at me. Rather the opposite, he would soothe me. But with his girlfriend, he would beat her black and blue and not an hour later apologize to her, bring her petty gifts  like flowers. And when I met her, I noticed how quiet she was and the way her gaze was always glued to the floor. She was slumped over and she looked empty, timid, and spoke very poorly of herself. This has taught me that abusers prey on people who have low self-esteem, people who aren't whole. And so before I enter a relationship, I know to ask myself if I am whole, otherwise, there is work to be done. I've learned that people aren't objects who I can or should try to fix. So I'll work on myself and I'll keep the image of her in my mind, so I don't allow anyone to step over my boundaries and don't become an abused person.

Danny

Get professional help in addition to your informal friends and family support system. There are really good organizations that help people get out of violent relationships, including Love Is Respect (https://www.loveisrespect.org/) and the National Domestic Violence Hotline (https://www.thehotline.org/).

If It's Your Friend Causing IPV

Telling a friend that they are being violent to their partner is something more people should be willing to do. It can feel hard and scary to confront someone who you think is doing harm. You may worry that they will turn around and do you harm through gossip or physically attacking you. You may feel sad at the idea of losing their friendship. But a person who is violent in their romantic or sexual relationships is not someone who you should maintain a friendship with, unless they are actively working to change their violent patterns. You can consider this from a make-the-world-a-better-place perspective, where you're not willing to lower your own standards of friendship to a person who commits IPV or you can consider it from a selfish place where you know someone who commits violence in a romantic relationship is likely to eventually spread that to their friends as well.

Carefully consider how you confront a friend who is being violent. Consider your safety and the safety of your friend's partner. How your friend takes the suggestion that they are violent with their partner has the potential to set off their violent tendencies. It can be helpful to pass this message on with the help of additional mutual friends. Hearing the message from multiple people at once will make it harder to ignore. You can also have the conversation in public, after having alerted your friend's partner, so they can find a safe place to be.

If It's Your Friend Experiencing IPV

One of the primary strategies of someone who is an abuser is separating their partner from their friends. This means that if your friend is being abused, their partner will probably try to come between you and your friend. You can't intervene directly, or your friend will push you away even harder. Instead, you can leave resources where they will find them (like this book or similar books, pamphlets, or websites), tell them that you will always be their friend, and keep showing up for them.

However, there may come a time when you are not able to help your friend. Your friend may push you away and not be willing to accept your help. You cannot force them to leave their abusive partner. In fact, trying to get your friend to leave the relationship may push your friend closer to their abusive partner. Your friend makes their own choices—and if they push you away over and over again, at some point you can't fight back against that.

Karen

One of my oldest and best friends was in a relationship with IPV when we were 19 and 20 years old and living together. It was one of the most difficult experiences of my life—and it remains a struggle between us. Even though we're still friends 20 years later, it was a serious rough patch for her and our friendship. I'm never quite sure if I can tell her the hard things she needs to hear, because she might threaten to end our relationship. If you have a friend experiencing IPV and aren't sure what to do, you aren't alone. There is probably not a perfect answer.

Violence Is Really Shitty and You Can Move Past It

Violence can make us feel shitty all the time, even when we're not currently experiencing it, even when we haven't experienced it in a long time, and even when it's us causing the violence. Give yourself space to heal from violence through therapy, meditation, time, friendships, new relationships, and nice long baths. And then, one day, you'll realize that you no longer feel shitty, and you haven't for a long time. Getting to that place takes work, and we know it's possible for you to do it.

When you're desperate to be loved, when you think no one can love you the way you are, when you think it's too hard to find love as an LGBTQ+ person— especially when you're nonbinary and you feel that no one will ever understand you, that no one will love you for the person you feel you are unless you pretend to be someone else—it's easy to cling to anyone who will show interest in you, even if you know that relationship is not in your best interest.
It's hard, but everyone wants to be loved, and so we might lower our standards. As a relationship becomes violent, we may feel trapped, like we have no choice but to stay with a violent person because that's the closest we may ever come to being loved, and it's even easier to feel this way when we struggle to be accepted by even our families.

Additional Resources

thetransbook.com/link/1201
Domestic Violence in the Transgender Community. Includes statistics, barriers, and a whole list of resources.

thetransbook.com/link/1202
National Resource Center on Domestic Violence resources on Sexual Assault and the Transgender Community.

thetransbook.com/link/1203
FORGE is an organization that provides resources for transgender and nonbinary people who have experienced relationship and sexual violence.

Here are a few resources if you are causing IPV:

thetransbook.com/link/1204
Can I Stop Being Abusive?

thetransbook.com/link/1205
The Day I Realised I Was An Emotional Abuser—But Can I Change?

thetransbook.com/link/1206
How to Stop Being Abusive to Your Partner

SEXY TIMES

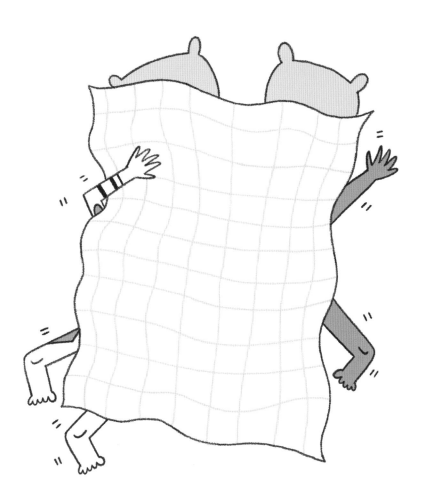

CHAPTER 13

DOING IT

Sex can look like a lot of different things, and figuring out how to connect physically with another person in ways that feel good to both people is important. This chapter discusses the many ways of being sexually active, especially for people who are transgender, nonbinary, and gender-fluid, including how to navigate language and partner communication.

Your Brain Is Where Sex Happens

There's a lot of conversation in this chapter about body parts and how they connect to sexual activities, and that conversation can be triggering because it relates to your body and your genitals. But the important thing to know as we're getting started is that the part of your body that is actually most closely related to your sexuality and your sexual activity is your brain. Your brain processes all of the senses around touch; it's what connects you to yourself and to other people; it's where you make decisions. You could have sex without any other part of your body, but you could not have sex without your brain.

Starting With Language

Talking about sex is a huge component of most sexual relationships, including talking about the specifics of your and your partner's bodies. Being able to name your body parts and describe to your partner what you want or don't want when you are engaging sexually together is a huge bonus. It helps tailor your sexual experiences to you specifically, your partner can ask questions that you can answer, and if something doesn't feel good or right, you can make that clear more easily. Ideally all of this happens without triggering even a flutter of dysphoria—because nothing kills a sexy mood like dysphoria.

Naming Your Body

You get to name your body parts. Whatever your body looks like, feels like, or acts like, whatever kinds of fluids your body creates, however your body likes to be touched, whatever the body parts of other people your body responds to, you get to name your own anatomy in ways that feel the sexiest and most authentic to you.

Maybe you pick a name that's thought of as a name—like Ari, Stevie, Glen, or Rory. You might pick words that are more descriptors than names—like Bunny, Little (or Big) Purple, or Ravisher. Or you could find words that feel real and authentic and don't really have any other kind of connotation to anyone—like Pundi, Sig, or Hund. You might pick words that describe anatomy closer to how you internally feel your body—like penis or clitoris. Or you could pick something else entirely to refer to your body parts. There's no reason, for example, that you couldn't pick a hand signal, a certain kind of humming noise, or a whistle to refer to specific parts of your body. You may even end up with a range of words to describe the same body part—some that are more loving and some that are a little more sexy. As many as you want, but they should work for you.

Ideally the names for your sexual anatomy will be something that makes you feel sexy, attractive, and attracted to your partner.

Communicating With Your Partner

You'll need to have a good conversation with your partner about language for your body that works for you because your partner won't have any way of knowing unless you tell them. This can be a hard moment because it means opening up to someone in very clearly personal ways. But it is also a great way to know if someone is going to be a good sexual partner for you.

The best way to start this conversation is probably by letting your partner know you have specific words (or sounds!) you'd like to use when the two of you talk about your body. Telling your partner can take many forms. You could do a show-and-tell. You could look at pictures where you've written in the words you use. You could write them an email. The point is that you let them know. They'll need to know.

So How DO Trans People Have Sex?

I wish this question had an immediate and obvious answer for everyone. But it doesn't, even for people trans, nonbinary, and gender-fluid, because it's not often part of what we see in media or even educational representations of sexual activities. The short answer is:

Trans and nonbinary people have sex the way everyone does.

While true, that's an explanation that would leave a lot of people with a lot of questions. So here's a slightly longer version:

All people have sex by mixing-and-matching their body parts with their partner's body parts in ways that (ideally) feel good to everyone.

But even that is not always enough. Our culture has shown us such a limited range of ways people are sexual it can sometimes be hard for people to think outside of that box. Our goal is for you to leave this chapter being able to imagine yourself being sexual in a happy, life-affirming way that speaks to your own individual patterns of love and attraction. So here are a few specific descriptions of how you may or may not be interested in being sexual with a partner:

- Kissing (mouth-to-mouth contact, sometimes including the tongue and sometimes not)

- Oral sex (mouth-to-genital contact, also sometimes called giving head, carpet munching, blow job, going down on)

- Anal sex (mouth-to-anus or genital-to-anus contact, also sometimes called butt sex, tossing salad, sodomy)

- Mutual masturbation (touching someone else's genitals with your hands or the other way around)

- Sex toys (using toys as a way to touch and stimulate your partner or the other way around)

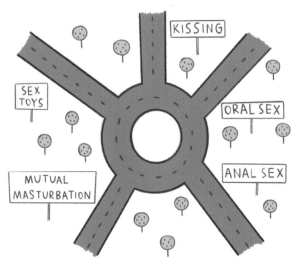

For some people, these activities can include your genitals— for others, they don't. Some people are not interested in any sexual activity that involves their genitals because it increases their sense of genital dysphoria, or they simply don't want their genitals touched at all.

You'll notice that all of these kinds of sexual activity are ones you can do regardless of your anatomy or your gender. Instead, it's all about what you want to do. Figuring out what kinds of sexual activities you want to do can be a process of trial-and-error. It may change over time—it is actually likely to change over time. As your body, relationships, emotions, knowledge, life circumstances, and so many other things change, what sexual activities speak to you and make you feel sexy and connected will also probably change. Paying attention to what activities you find fun, sexy, arousing, and pleasurable is the road map to what kinds of sexual activities are for you.

Let's Talk Orgasms

Orgasms are (usually) perks of sexual activity, and they are not necessary for the sexual activity to be fun, engaging, and fulfilling. In fact, some people aren't so into them. This is particularly true for people with substantial genital dysphoria. For people who do enjoy orgasm, it is often cited as one of the best feelings in the body. Orgasms are rhythmic contractions of the muscles in and around the genitals, including the bladder, anus, and other internal organs that many people do not associate with sexual arousal. Whether you and/or your partner want to orgasm and ejaculate should be an important part of your conversations about your sexual activities.

One potential part of an orgasm experience is ejaculation, which is when fluid is pushed out of the genitals due to the rhythmic contractions. You should have conversations with your partner about whether you ejaculate, and you should learn if they ejaculate.

Here are some useful things to know about ejaculation:

- Some people ejaculate when they have an orgasm and some people don't. This is true regardless of their anatomy.

- Hormone therapy can change how people ejaculate, in both the amount and the kind of fluid, how ejaculation feels, and they might even stop ejaculating altogether.

- The refractory period, which is the amount of time after an ejaculation before the next erection and arousal cycle begin, can lengthen.

The final point: orgasms should be fun! They should be for yourself and your partner to bring you closer together—and if they aren't doing that for you, it's okay to leave them out of your sexual activities.

Kathryn

As with most things in your life, the kinds of people and the kinds of ways you want to have sex (or not!) will change. What is important at every stage is finding ways to talk with your partner about the ways you do and don't want to go about doing it with each other. Sometimes you'll be able to have these conversations out loud, and other times you'll feel awkward, so texting or messaging each other might feel safer. It doesn't matter how these conversations happen, but it does matter that you and your partner are getting your needs met in a way that works for both of you.

Let's Talk Pain

Sometimes sex is painful—psychologically, physically, or both. Regardless of the cause or type of pain, stop what you're doing and assess why you're in pain.

Psychological Pain

This is, most commonly for trans people, dysphoria. Because being sexual is such a bodily intimate activity, if your body is causing you dysphoria, sexual activity will likely make that worse. Be open with your partner about what's going on and why you may not be able to be sexual with them, either in a given moment or over a period of time or maybe even ever. There are many ways to be close with someone other than sexual activities, so find ones that work for the two of you rather than putting distance between you because you aren't comfortable being sexual. You may find you enjoy touching your partner during times when your dysphoria is getting in the way of you enjoying your own body being touched sexually.

Physical Pain

People can experience physical pain before, during, or after sex for a lot of reasons. There are some rumors out there that physical pain is just part of having sex—especially when being penetrated. But it's not true! There is no sex act that is inherently painful, even the first time someone is penetrated (anally or vaginally).

Here are some of the most common causes of pain surrounding sex, as well as a little bit of information about each:

- **Going too fast**—People's bodies sometimes need time to warm up. This could be an issue during vaginal or anal penetration that you're feeling nervous about. While it may be hard to slow down to make sure you have enough water, or silicone-based lubricant, or when you're nervous—that's when it's absolutely the most important. Penetration pain can spiral and become increasingly painful over time if you don't take the time to pay attention when it first gets started. Make sure you talk with your partner, and that the two of you are on the same page. Your partner should be prepared to stop should you need to.

- **Recovery from surgery**—Whenever you have surgery on any part of your body, there is a recovery period where you'll need to be gentle with your body and possibly refrain from sexual activity. This is especially true of genital surgery. There are some genital surgeries (like phalloplasty) that may result in pain during erections for the rest of your life. But most genital surgeries (including vaginoplasty) will heal and should not cause you pain if healed correctly. This is something to talk with your doctor about and follow their post-surgical instructions, including when you are able to engage in sexual activity again, very closely.

- **Accidents**—Things happen during sex. You can roll off a bed, move your fingers the wrong way, not quite have your pelvis lined up with your partner's, and more. As long as you are in open communication with your partner about how you're feeling and how they're feeling, these can be taken in stride.

Of course, the connection between our bodies and our minds (between the physical and the psychological) is deep. So if you are experiencing psychological pain, it may well feel like physical pain. When someone describes a breakup with someone they are in love with as having a broken heart, their emotional pain is causing physical pain. The same is true around issues of dysphoria. That pain may be very physical in the way that you feel it—and that pain is real, not imagined. Brain scans have verified that emotional hurt can cause the sensors that take note of physical pain to light up. But fixing this kind of pain requires a different kind of approach, because you have to address the psychological or emotional disruptions to help the physical pain get better. You will definitely need a therapist, probably in addition to other doctors, to help with this kind of pain.

Other Kinds of Pain

There are kinds of pain some people find sexually pleasurable—sexy, consensual pain. These kinds of activities can include things like pulling hair or scratching someone's back. They can also include more intense sensations that might fall under the umbrella of BDSM (Bondage and Discipline, Dominance and Submission, and Sadism and Masochism). This kind of sexual activity usually requires a lot of knowledge about boundaries and a high level of self-control. Learning how to engage in BDSM safely requires classes and education. We usually encourage people under 18 who are aroused by BDSM activities to primarily stick to fantasizing about it. After they turn 18, they are able to access education and learning experiences that will provide them with safe ways to engage in BDSM.

Not all BDSM and other intentional pain during sex is good. Sometimes, when someone is in a lot of psychological pain, it becomes too much to bear. In response, people start to inflict physical pain on themselves as a way to make their internal pain "real." Some common examples of this are cutting, scratching, or burning the skin. Another example is hurting themselves sexually. This can include having sex with people they know are hurtful to them, leaving themselves at risk of STIs, and engaging in painful sexual activities as a form of self-harm rather than as a source of sexual pleasure.

If you find yourself engaging in sexual activities that are pain-inducing, either psychologically or physically, think about whether you are truly doing these things as a kind of sexy activity or as a form of self-harm. And if the kinds of sex you are engaging in (or considering) feel painful in an abusive way, revisit Chapter 12 to learn more about how to deal with this kind of relationship violence.

Solo Sex?

It's perfectly fine and normal to have complicated feelings about masturbation.

Is masturbation sex? We say yes! It involves many of the same kinds of touch and stimulation that partnered sex has but differs in its emotional connection. During partnered sex, the emotions are between the people engaging in the sexual activity. During masturbation, though, the person has the potential to connect with themselves, to create their body and the specifics of the sexual activity in their imagination. Masturbation can be healing and boost your sense of self. Here are a few tips and suggestions that can increase that possibility:

- It's okay for your body to give you pleasure, even when it isn't formed in a way you feel represents you.
- Go slow.
- Explore, figure out what feels good.
- There is no right way to do it.

Finding out what feels good by yourself can be safer and less dysphoric, and that can allow you to communicate these details to a partner.

Karen

Masturbation can be a very different experience from partnered sex, and for most people it fulfills a different need. So, while we do consider masturbation a kind of sex, it's different from most other kinds of sex. For example, it's not cheating on your partner. Because it is about your relationship with yourself, it is a special, unique element that can be done along with your partner but can also be something that is just for you.

Reclaiming and Claiming Sexual Pleasure

We talk very little about sexual pleasure in our culture, but we talk a whole lot about sex, which is a little odd. But that doesn't mean your attention has to be divided. Instead, be sure that your sexual activities and the associated conversations you have about sex include pleasure as a key element. For most people, most of the time, sex is about pleasure.

Sometimes I think we can forget, as LGBT people, that we are allowed to like sex and enjoy it like any other kind of couple. I personally tend to think about sex less in terms of gender, and more in terms of the role you take on. I remember with my first girlfriend—before I found out I was a gay man—even though we weren't sexually active, we still discussed what that might've looked like in the future. I mentioned that I liked being a bit more dominant in those 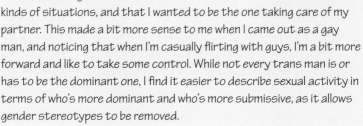 kinds of situations, and that I wanted to be the one taking care of my partner. This made a bit more sense to me when I came out as a gay man, and noticing that when I'm casually flirting with guys, I'm a bit more forward and like to take some control. While not every trans man is or has to be the dominant one, I find it easier to describe sexual activity in terms of who's more dominant and who's more submissive, as it allows gender stereotypes to be removed.

Luka

Additional Resources

 thetransbook.com/link/1301
"How I Lost My Virginity as a Transgender Woman"
This is a true story of how one trans woman lost her virginity. It's often useful to read about someone else's experiences—even if yours ends up (or has already been) very different.

 thetransbook.com/link/1302
"11 Sex Tips From (and for) Trans People"
These eleven tips are concrete and accessible.

CHAPTER 14

SAFER SEX

Pregnancy and STI prevention—from hormonal methods to condoms to PrEP and PEP (medications that prevent HIV from taking hold in the body)—are critical pieces of the sexy sexual activity puzzle. This chapter includes concrete information and encouragement for how to incorporate safety into all of the sexual activities from Chapter 13. That chapter was probably a lot more fun to read than this one, but this one can save your life.

Many of the conversations about safer sex refer to specific body parts and specific gametes and fluids. Be sure to attend to self-care, and if you need to step away because these conversations make you feel uncomfortable or dysphoric, that's okay. Just come back to this chapter before you are sexual in ways that can put your sexual health at risk.

Safer vs. Safe

Doctors, nurses, educators, and others used to talk about the importance of having "safe sex" by using condoms and birth control. But really, saying that kind of sex is "safe" is giving false promises. Condoms and other forms of birth control fail sometimes. It is definitely safer to use them, but we just can't guarantee perfect—or completely safe—in anything.

We now talk about how sexual activities can be safer. These are ways sexual contact can be less physically risky, less likely to contribute to STIs or unplanned pregnancies. Taking these steps matter. They will improve your sexual health and your partner's sexual health. The methods to reduce pregnancies and STIs are medically tested and highly effective.

Pregnancy Prevention

Often called birth control or contraception (it is against "contra" birth "conception"). We'll stick with the word contraception for this chapter because it's a little more medically accurate.

Sometimes trans people, especially trans people who are on hormones, think they don't need to use birth control. They assume the replacement hormones are preventing their body from creating gametes, but that's just not always the case. If you don't want you or your partner to become pregnant, you definitely should not have the kind of sex that can produce a pregnancy without using pregnancy prevention methods. To prevent pregnancy, a contraceptive method must be used during penis in vagina sex, regardless of the gender identities of the people involved and regardless of whether the intent is for the penis to ejaculate or not.

The four basic kinds of contraception are:

- hormones
- barriers
- behaviors
- surgery

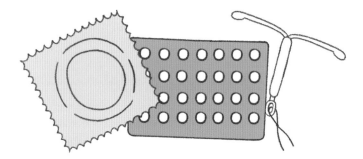

Last year I did a research project about the many, many negative effects of abstinence-only sex education, and I think I learned more doing that project than I have throughout the entirety of the sex ed curriculum I've received during my four years in public school. It's not like I did an impressive amount of research or anything, it's just that my school set a low bar. In eighth grade, we got about four weeks of riveting information about the length of a pregnancy, dynamic diagrams of penises and vaginas, and stern warnings about how, if you have sex, you too could become a sex offender. Good times.

What they didn't teach us in my sex ed class was anything about . . . sex. I think they told us that a penis goes in a vagina, nine months go by, and then boom: there's a baby. But that's all. No mention of different kinds of sex. No mention of queer sex or relationships. No mention of protection—except when they told us that condoms weren't going to be completely effective, so we just shouldn't have sex.

And look, maybe it doesn't matter. I feel like I know what I need to know about having safer sex, but I wish I didn't have to Google everything and find out on my own. I wish we had been able to talk about sex and the feelings that go along with it. I wish we had covered trans+ issues and how to deal with dysphoria during sex. I wish everyone were able to receive accurate, comprehensive, informative, diverse sexual education, because I know I would have been a lot less confused if I had.

E.

Hormonal Prevention

Hormonal prevention works by changing the hormones in a person's body so eggs are not produced and to reduce the potential for reproduction by making the fallopian tube and uterine environments less hospitable to either kind of gamete. The most common (although not the most effective) form of hormonal contraception is the birth control pill. The most effective kinds are called LARCs, or Long-Acting Reversible Contraceptives, including IUDs and the implant. Some trans men and nonbinary people are not enthusiastic about using hormonal contraception because it increases the female hormones in their body, which can increase chest growth and hip growth. Other trans men and nonbinary people appreciate that hormonal contraception can stop their periods entirely.

Barrier Prevention

Barrier prevention works by putting a barrier made of latex (or another material) between the two kinds of gametes. The most common form is the external condom. It goes on a penis and catches the semen. It is used during penetrative sex in a vagina or anus or during oral sex. Internal condoms can be put inside the vagina or the anus.

Some trans women and nonbinary people are uncomfortable with the genital contact that comes with putting barrier methods of contraception on or in their bodies. In these cases, a partner can support them by being in charge of putting the contraception on or in their partner's body.

Behavioral Contraception

Behavioral contraception is about making choices related to sexual activity to reduce the likelihood of STIs and pregnancy. When using behavioral contraception, preventing pregnancy is easier than preventing STI. There is only one way for pregnancy to occur: when two gametes of different kinds meet up. And there is only one way that sexual activity can result in this: when a penis is inside a vagina. If you avoid this specific sexual activity, you will be avoiding pregnancy. While avoiding penis-in-vagina sex is often referred to as abstinence, that assumes a pretty narrow perspective on what sex really is. There are many other ways to have sex and to be sexual beyond penis-in-vagina sex. The other kinds of behavioral contraception are the pull-out method (or withdrawal) and natural family planning. Withdrawal is often laughed about as not being very effective, but when the person with the penis always takes their penis out of their partner before nearing orgasm, it actually works pretty well. Problems arise when the person tries to get as close to orgasm as possible before pulling out, and then they ejaculate without meaning to. Natural family planning is a relatively complex way of keeping very close track of ovulation and fertilization in a person with ovaries and eggs. It involves a lot of very close contact with the genitals and reproductive system, and so most trans and nonbinary people are not interested in using it. If you would like more information, it is readily available online.

Surgical Contraception

Surgical contraception is less common for most young people. It is more common for trans youth because they may be seeking these surgeries for reasons beyond pregnancy prevention, to bring their bodies into alignment with their gender identities. Chapter 8 discusses the surgeries that some trans and nonbinary people access. The surgeries related to removing gamete production from the body (hysterectomies, orchiectomies, for example) are the ones that are relevant to pregnancy prevention.

Karen

There are so many ways of preventing pregnancy! Don't feel that you have to stick with just one method. Instead, you can play around with them to find out what works most effectively for you and your partner. Each type has pros and cons, and it's not always clear whether the pros outweigh the cons for you until you've given it a try. Doctors aren't always able to take their time helping you figure out which one will be best for you, so do your own reading and be your own advocate if what you're currently using isn't working for you.

STI Prevention

STIs can be transmitted in many ways, so preventing transmission is more complicated than preventing unwanted pregnancies.

There are three kinds of STIs:

- **Bacterial STIs** can, almost always, be treated and cured. They often do not have any symptoms, which is why it is so important to get tested. The most common bacterial STIs are gonorrhea, chlamydia, and syphilis, and as of 2018 they are all on the rise.

- **Viral STIs** are not curable, although sometimes the body clears the virus itself. Viral STIs can be treated so they are less likely to be transmitted to another person and so the harm to the body is reduced as much as possible. The most common viral STIs are Human Papillomavirus (HPV), Herpes (HSV), Hepatitis B, Human Immunodeficiency Virus (HIV), and Vaginitis (including Bacterial Vaginosis, Yeast, etc.). There is growing awareness of Cytomegalovirus (CMV) as well.

- **Parasitic infections** can be treated and cured. They are usually just uncomfortable and don't pose any real risk to the infected person. The most common parasitic STIs are Pubic Lice (sometimes called crabs) and Scabies.

Here is a list of the ways STIs can be transmitted:

- skin-to-skin contact
- semen (whether the semen includes sperm or not, it can include STIs)
- vaginal lubrication
- rectal fluids
- blood (including sharing IV drug needles)
- breastmilk
- prenatal transmission

Before you get too worried about all the different ways to transmit STIs, remember that if a person does not have an STI in their body, they can't transmit it. So, if two people are having sex, and they have both been tested and know they do not have an STI, neither of them will contract an STI, regardless of what sexual activities they engage in with each other, as long as they are not engaging sexually with anyone else. The issue is that most people haven't had a full STI screening, and so they are less aware of their current STI status.

Here is a list of the ways to prevent STIs:

- **Barrier methods**—Barrier methods must be either latex; a synthetic latex alternative, like polyisoprene, polyurethane, or polyethylene; or a natural animal product like lambskin. They prevent almost all STIs when used correctly, except STIs that are transmitted through skin-to-skin contact.

- **Immunizations**—These are shots that prevent a virus from infecting the body. They currently exist for Hepatitis and HPV. Immunizations are in development for Herpes and HIV.

- **PrEP and PEP**—These are medications that prevent HIV from taking hold in the body. More information on both of these kinds of prevention methods is in the next section.

- **Behavioral methods**—Reducing the risk of contracting an STI can mean a lot of different things, and behavior obviously plays a role. Using a condom and taking PrEP, for example, are behaviors that reduce the risk of STIs. But this section is particularly about understanding what kinds of STIs you may be at highest risk for and reducing that risk by taking specific actions or refraining from specific kinds of sexual contact.

Being PrEP-ed and PEP-y

PrEP and PEP are relatively new medications that work to prevent the spread of HIV. People who are transgender have a much higher rate of HIV infection when compared to the general population, which is why we are focusing specifically on this STI. HIV is also more complex—from the virus itself to the testing and the treatment—than most other STIs. So before we get into PrEP and PEP (and ART), here is a quick overview of the virus itself:

HIV stands for the Human Immunodeficiency Virus. This virus is particularly tricky because it gets into the body's immune system cells and turns them into HIV replicating cells rather than immune system replicating cells. Over time, this means the body has fewer and fewer immune system cells and more and more HIV cells. Without a strong immune system, the body can't fight off other illnesses. When the immune system has dropped to a certain level, the person is diagnosed with AIDS, which stands for Acquired ImmunoDeficiency Syndrome. This is a signal that the person can't fight off illnesses that are usually easier to recover from.

This brings us to ART, PrEP, and PEP.

- **ART**—A medication that targets retroviruses, such as HIV. Antiretroviral therapy (ART) drugs do not cure the virus, but, when taken in combination, can slow the disease progression by preventing the growth of the virus. ART has the potential to reduce the virus in a person's body so much that it is undetectable (or not able to be found) in their blood and sexual fluids. So if a person living with HIV is following their medication regimen exactly as prescribed, it is very unlikely they will give the virus to someone.

- **PEP**—Post-exposure prophylaxis is a medication that is taken as soon as possible, but no later than 72 hours, after potential exposure to HIV. PEP is very effective, but not 100%. Its effectiveness is dependent on how soon after exposure the medication is initiated.

- **PrEP**—Pre-exposure prophylaxis is a medication that is taken daily to reduce the chances of contracting HIV. When taken correctly, reduction is estimated to be at least 90% for sexual contact and 70% for IV drug use. People who know they are at risk for HIV exposure and who take the proactive step toward taking PrEP have a substantially reduced likelihood of contracting HIV.

Between these three drugs, new HIV infections have declined significantly in the last century. Particularly the combination of ART and PrEP, along with condoms, means people who are HIV negative and who are in relationships with people who are HIV positive are very unlikely to contract HIV. Studies have shown that the number might even be as little as zero, as long as everyone is taking their medication as they should be!

But How Well Does Prevention Work?

Some methods work really, really well. Others work not so well. Some methods of prevention are right and useful for you, and others are not. Consider the following factors when deciding on prevention methods:

- What are you trying to prevent? Pregnancy? STIs? If so, which ones?

- Do you or your partner have access to a medical professional to prescribe access to your safer sex method of choice?

- How might your safer sex method of choice interact with your or your partner's gender, including steps toward medical transitioning?

- How effective is any specific contraceptive?

Here is a handy chart for figuring out some of this information.

For the rest of it, you'll need to talk with your partner and potentially others (like a healthcare worker) as well.

Contraceptives

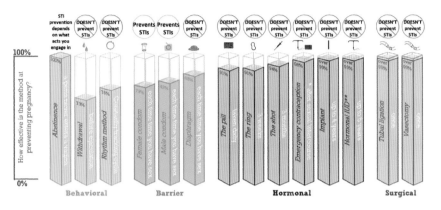

www.unhushed.org
Reprinted with permission.

Talking With Your Partner

The most effective way to reduce risks associated with sexual contact may be the least medical and the most mundane: Talk with your partner. Open communication where you both share your worries, fears, hopes, and expectations is what will make the biggest difference. Go together to get tested for STIs. Share your experiences with your body so your partner will know if it's acting abnormally in any way.

Starting this conversation isn't always easy—especially when you have been having sex for some time, maybe weeks or months or even years—and you haven't stopped to talk about safer sex. Or maybe you did before the first time you had sex, but you haven't talked about it since then.

But there's good news: Now is a great time to start a conversation! Tell them you've been reading a book, and it talks about how important safer sex is and how the conversation needs to continue rather than happen just once before a couple becomes sexually active. Good things will hopefully come from that dialogue.

But if your partner is upset by the idea of talking about safer sex, then it might be time to reconsider your relationship with your partner. Everyone, whether they are sexually active or not, needs to be engaged in making sure that they and their partner are sexually healthy. If the person you are having sex with (or considering having sex with) is not highly concerned with both your and their sexual health, that is a warning sign. Head back to Chapter 12.

Sexual Health Is Forever

Making sure your body is as right for you as it can be is a big part of what this book is about. One of the ways you can do that is by taking care of your sexual health. It will make a huge difference for the rest of your life, because sexual health lasts forever. As a summary, here are the things we recommend you do:

- Make thoughtful decisions about with whom and under what circumstances you want to be sexually active.
- Regularly and consistently use safer sex methods like condoms and other STI and pregnancy prevention methods.
- Have sexual health visits with medical professionals, including STI testing, on an annual or biannual basis, depending on your sexual activity level.

By taking this advice, you'll be able to have your body functioning, healthy, and well taken care of, for the rest of your life.

Additional Resources

thetransbook.com/link/1401
Safer Sex by Planned Parenthood
Planned Parenthood is the go-to resource for STI education, protection, testing, and treatment in many parts of the United States.

thetransbook.com/link/1402
The STD Project: Breaking the Stigma
A huge repository of information about STIs, including facts, resources, testing, prevention, and support. This site is run by a woman who talks openly about her STI and her experience having an STI.

LIFE

CHAPTER 15

FAMILY

People usually think of their families as the people who parent them and their siblings, along with grandparents, cousins, aunts, and uncles. The people in our families often have very clear hopes and dreams for who we are and who we will become. Sometimes those hopes and dreams get in the way of them seeing, loving, and supporting us for who we are. This chapter is all about navigating that process.

Who's Your Family?

People feel differently about who they consider to be their family—and who they consider to be their important family. Most people think of the adults who raised them when they were babies, children, and teenagers as family. But if these people are not understanding or supportive of you, sometimes it is important to move away from them.

Family of Origin

This is the first kind of family: the kind you were birthed into. These people are really luck-of-the-draw. Sometimes they're great. Sometimes they're terrible. Usually they are somewhere in between. Most people have at least someone in their family of origin who they connect with, whether it's a parent or grandparent or sibling.

Your family of origin will have a substantial impact on who you are, because they're the ones who taught you about being a person when you were small. They showed you what it was like to be in relationships with someone else, including the ways you can and should expect to be spoken to, touched, and loved. They are the ones who have told you whether or not you are worthy of being respected and treated well, both because of how they treated you and how they treated each other. These messages are often given and internalized before a person is even out of diapers.

Karen

This idea that your family creates important parts of who you are and how you connect with others is called attachment theory. The idea of this theory is that your first glimpse and experience of a relationship with your parent shapes how you understand and engage in relationships for the rest of your life. Even if you didn't have a great experience with relationships early on, you can still learn how to have them later in life. It takes attention and work, usually with someone who understands attachment theory in adolescence and adulthood.

Whether a family of origin is supportive of their fellow trans and nonbinary members or not is one of the largest factors impacting whether a young trans or nonbinary person feels confident in their identity. If your family is not supportive of you, that is not your fault.

Family of Choice

This is the second kind of family: the kind that becomes family over time because of how they treat you and how you want to spend your time supporting each other.

Families of choice are often created out of a community or group of friends and all of you are tied to each other. Families of choice usually like and love each other, although, as with a family of birth, you will probably like some of them more than others. But you are all able to rely on each other when things aren't going well and you are accepted not in spite of your gender identity but because of it.

I am so, so lucky to have a supportive family and to not have to worry about getting disowned, kicked out, or abused for being gay. My heart goes out to all those who are not in the same situation, and I am very grateful to have the parents I do. Though I have no physical consequences to worry about, things still aren't easy. I may never fully come out to my parents because they don't understand LGBTQ+ issues and they have not been open to learning about them.

Any time I bring up sexual orientations or gender identities other than gay, lesbian, straight, bi, cis, or binary trans, my dad's immediate response is "Y'all doin' too much." Pansexual? "Y'all doin' too much." Aromantic? "Y'all doin' too much." Gender-fluid? "Y'all doin' too much." My mom isn't much better. Whenever I mention trans+ people who are also attracted to the same gender they identify as, my mom will say something along the lines of: "What's the point of being trans+ if you're just going to be gay anyway?" Though I don't believe my parents have any malicious intent when they say these things, their statements certainly don't make me feel any more comfortable with my confusing, complicated identity issues.

I know I'm not the only one in this situation. I think there are a lot of people whose parents are not homophobic, but are homo-ignorant. Though the immediate consequences of coming out are unquestionably less for people like me, having parents who are unwilling to see certain LGBTQ+ identities as anything other than a joke or a quirk still hurts.

E.

What Your Family May Mean to You

Your family—either of birth or of choice—may be your world. Or they may be what you fall back on. Or they may not play a huge role in your life. Your family may be your first call when something big happens or you may not even bother to tell them anything. You may love them so much it hurts or feel relatively ambivalent about them. There isn't a "wrong" way to do family. What's important is that you feel seen and accepted for who you are, whether by your family or by other people.

Family Dynamics

Obviously, families are complex. Figuring out who your family is, how close you want to be with them, and how they can support you, are questions you have to consider. Sometimes thinking through what you would like your answers to these questions to be can help you figure out what your answers to these questions actually are. Pulling away from your family of origin is almost always a painful thing that feels like a loss. Knowing what a healthy family dynamic can and should look like is usually the first step to understanding whether yours is one worth putting time and energy into to help it be stronger.

The details of a healthy family can run the gamut. Sometimes families are big, sometimes they're little. But there are some things that are really important to a healthy family and can't be ignored. People in healthy families:

- **trust each other.** While they may not choose to share all of the details of their lives, family members know they can call on each other when needed.

- **treat each other with respect and kindness.** They interact with openness and interest in what the other person is experiencing in their life. They don't call each other names or unfairly place blame.

- **spend time together.** This doesn't always mean in person or over the holidays like the movies say you should. Spending time together can mean everything from texting silly GIFs to baking cookies. The important thing is that you show each other you care through the ways you choose to spend your time.

- **fight sometimes.** It's easy to think that if you're fighting, there are problems. But disagreeing with someone doesn't mean your relationship with them is unhealthy. Instead, it's about how you treat each other when you disagree.

- **don't always understand each other, but they always want to.** This is particularly important to think about as it relates to your gender identity. Your family might not understand when you come out to them, but they will continue to love you and will work toward understanding you.

So what does it mean if your family of origin isn't a healthy family? Well, it can mean a lot of different things. It can mean that it's time for you to find a family of choice. Or that you should find a therapist or ask that your entire family go to therapy together. For some people, it is really hard to realize that their family dynamic isn't a healthy one, while others have known for as long as they can remember. Either way, the health of your family of origin is not the way it is because of anything you have done. As one of the children (as opposed to parents or other adults) in the family, you came into the family. As a teenager, you may have some influence over the family dynamics, but you cannot control them. Your primary work at this stage of your life is to understand and learn to take care of yourself. If you find yourself in an unhealthy family, put your head down, stay under the radar, and survive until you're a legal adult. At that point, you may be able to move out and find ways to support yourself.

Coming Out to Your Family

The process of coming out to your family can be one of the most anxiety-inducing things you do during your transition. There are the usual questions of whether or not they'll accept you, whether they'll understand what trans or nonbinary actually means, and if they'll ask you a bunch of uncomfortable questions.

As you consider when and how you want to come out to your family, revisit Chapter 3 to make sure you're as prepared as possible. One of the first steps is making sure you have come to know yourself and feel comfortable with who you know yourself to be. Being as certain as possible about your identity is going to help your family see that you are serious. You'll also want to weigh the risks and benefits of coming out to make sure you are as safe as possible, and decide the best time and place to tell your family members.

After you've come out, even if your family is accepting, they'll likely need a lot of time to adjust to your name and pronouns as well as having the knowledge that you're trans or nonbinary. If possible, find a friend or trusted adult who you can confide in about your frustrations and successes as time goes by. It will help you feel less alone.

Your Name and Pronouns

Recognizing your name and pronouns might be hard for your family. They have spent years thinking about you in a certain way and now all of those thought patterns have to be broken and rebuilt. Most families need a little bit of time after someone comes out to grapple with the idea that the name and pronouns they have used were wrong and have changed. Before you make assumptions about whether your family is accepting of you or not, give them a month or two after you've come out. While some families might have suspected your gender identity before you came out and others are exceptionally open and accepting, most will need a little time.

If, after a few months, your family struggles to use your correct name and pronouns, but they seem to really be trying, let them know you understand that they're working on it. Tell them you know they'll mess up sometimes and will keep getting better. You can choose whether to correct them every time they mess up or only every few times—but trust that they'll get their language in order over time and with your continued nudges.

However, some families aren't accepting. After a few months, these families either won't seem to be trying or won't seem to care about your name or pronouns. This is an entirely different kind of issue. Your family ignoring who you are hurts because it is a kind of emotional and psychological violence. You are likely not the right person to tell them these things. If this is the situation you find yourself in, you have a few options and a last-ditch survival strategy. Here are the options for educating your family:

- Ask if they will see a therapist with a specialty in gender identity and trans topics with you.
- Ask if they will find someone from your local PFLAG group to talk with.
- Ask if they will read a book that you can recommend about gender identity.
- If you have another adult advocate who you know is supportive and who your family trusts, ask if your family will talk with the adult advocate.

But if you've tried all these approaches and your family is still ignoring and hurting you, it may be time to go into survival mode. You may need to find a different place to live, with people who understand and see you and your identity. You may need to find a job and try to move out and support yourself before you turn 18 or before you finish high school. You may need to prioritize your own survival. We wish no one ever had to make this choice, but we know that is not the world that we live in. If this is the path you find yourself on, we hope you will do so with the knowledge and support of friends, teachers, and other adults who understand your dilemma and will serve as sounding boards for you making choices that are safe.

Coming out to my family members was one of the toughest things I've ever done, and I was met with many different reactions throughout the process. Luckily, my parents and my sister were completely supportive of my transition, and as I have grown from it I have become closer to them than I have ever been before.

When I decided to come out to my mom's side of the family, I was met with the same support, but I definitely had to do more explaining than with my immediate family, since many of them weren't as well versed with the trans experience. For the most part, they were respectful and supportive of my decision, which is something I will always be grateful for.

Things ended up being a little more dicey when it came to my dad's side of the family, though. They are definitely more old school and conservative than my mom's side, and most of them have never had any experience dealing with, or even being exposed to, trans people. Because of this, after I found out I was trans, I avoided that side of the family out of fear of being rejected. I put off coming out to them for a long time, until my dad finally ended up telling them while I was off at school. According to my dad, it was a little more of a mixed reaction than with my mom's side, with it being unclear if they truly understood what it meant for me to come out as transgender. Even though I am technically out to my dad's side of the family now, I still avoid them out of fear. Even though I love them and want to visit them, I can't help feeling a tightness in my chest at the thought of seeing them again.

Drace

My family is made up of Mexican immigrants who came from small pueblos where everyone knew one another and their shortcomings. My mother came from a poor family; she lived in a humble stone house with no windows or doors, a family of farmers. My father came from a pueblo with better houses and actual roads; they would slaughter pigs and sell the meat in the plaza. To say the least, they came from a place where machismo is prominent and LGBT people were just "non-existent." And as it goes, my parents eventually met, immigrated to the United States, and had me. As my mom gazed into my tiny face, she couldn't help but pin all her dreams onto me. Of course, my life turned out different from the one she fantasized for me. And for that, I broke her heart.

My coming out was not easy for her to comprehend. She told me that she felt as if I had died. Of course, emotional 13-year-old me couldn't understand what that meant, and those words stung more than anything. And so those words rang in my ears for the next four years. As I grew older, my parents gradually became better at tolerating my transition of ftm. I also became more mature and empathetic; as I watched documentaries of people like me I realized that feeling is very common among parents, even the supportive ones. One day, I realized what she wanted to tell me about all of those dreams she had for me: they were gone in an instant. That day a wall came down as I began to understand her perspective. Although we have a long way to go, I've never been closer to her.

Danny

Your Gender Expression

Because of some cultural quirk, many families are more accepting of a range of gender expressions than they are gender identities. You'll probably find that your family is comfortable with you having a freer range of motion in your gender expression than they are your name or your pronouns. This is most true if you identify as a man or as masc. Our culture continues to value masculine traits over feminine traits, and so encourages people who are typically labeled as "girl" to do things like wearing jeans and playing sports and having short hair.

If you are someone who identifies as a woman or femme and your family expected you to identify as a man or masc, they are more likely to struggle with your gender expression. It is less accepted for people who are assumed to be a man to do things like wear a dress, express their emotions, and express themselves through other typically "feminine" forms.

And even so, it is still typically more accepted to push your range of gender expression than it is to openly identify as trans or nonbinary.

Families Can Be Beautiful

And they should be beautiful. If that hasn't been your experience, know there is a magical place where you will be able to find your family. They'll have games and gardening or golf and garlic bread or glitter and gouda or whatever hobbies and foods you love on the ready for you to celebrate your achievements and grieve your losses. They'll stand by you and know you for who you truly are. For those of you who don't have that yet, the magical place where your family lives is the future—and it is getting closer every day. You may have to be patient (which is no small task), but you can always dream of what it will look like.

Additional Resources

Your family may benefit from reading about gender identity and how to support the trans and gender-nonbinary teenagers in their lives (like you!). Here is a list of suggestions to offer to them:

thetransbook.com/link/1501
The nation's largest family and ally organization.

thetransbook.com/link/1502
A list of resources with lots of videos of parent and family testimonies.

thetransbook.com/link/1503
Lots of resources on raising gender expansive kids, along with information in various languages.

thetransbook.com/link/1504
An article with a surprising piece of advice: Listen to your kids—they know what feels right and true to them.

thetransbook.com/link/1505
This reading list from PFLAG isn't youth-specific but includes so many great books and resources for families we couldn't leave it out.

thetransbook.com/link/1506
Contains a lot of downloadable content for parents and families.

And you may benefit from having resources on how to support and work with your family. Here is a list of resources for you:

thetransbook.com/link/1507
Has a section at the end for what to do when you don't have family support.

thetransbook.com/link/1508
This website has some resources for coming out to family.

thetransbook.com/link/1509
A PDF resource from the UK that includes a section on coming out to family, among other topics.

thetransbook.com/link/1510
A quick PDF brochure about coming out to family.

CHAPTER 16

SCHOOL

ust as a person's family can either be a safe haven or a scary place, so can school. In this chapter, we dive into the ways schools can either be a place of support or a place where it hurts to be. We'll also talk about advocacy in schools—tools you and your cis friends can use to make things better—around issues like bathrooms, locker rooms, and coming out.

Who's on Your Team?

Your school's ecosystem, or all of the people and systems and laws and policies at your school, plays a huge role in what your experiences are there. You'll probably find that some pieces of the ecosystem work in your favor and some of them don't. Maybe your school has some pretty great policies about bathrooms, but those come from the school district or even the state, and the actual people in your school are neither welcoming nor inclusive. Or maybe there's a really inclusive culture among most of your peers (even the ones who you don't personally like), and that's a huge difference from the teachers and administration who are not part of that culture. It's rare to be in a school that's either all welcoming or all problematic. So figuring out who is there to support and advocate with and for you is a critical first step to figuring out how to be trans or nonbinary in your school. Here are a few ways to start that process:

- Keep a sharp eye out for welcoming rainbow stickers on teachers' and counselors' doors. These are often used as a signal to students who need a place to feel safe.

- If you know anyone else who is out about their gender identity, start by talking with them. Who have they found at the school to be supportive? Which specific groups of friends, teachers, clubs, or administrators offer a place of refuge when it's needed? Can they give you an introduction if you don't already know the supportive people in your school?

- Is there a GSA at your school? If so, how can you find out if they are welcoming to people who are trans and non-binary, in addition to people who are lesbian, gay, and bisexual?

- Is there any education about gender identity in your school? If so, who provides it? How might you find out if it's inclusive of you?

Finding the right people to back you up as you come out and navigate the school will provide you with a safe space from which to venture out into uncharted territory—and somewhere to retreat if you need it.

Some schools won't have a safe place in them. If that's the kind of school you are attending, find a place outside of school that can serve that role for you. That might be your home and family, it might be a local LGBTQ+ center, or it might be an online community. There is a safe space for you in this world and finding it will help to fortify you and help you be stronger in places that are not safe.

Choosing Your School

Sometimes you will get to choose where you spend your time— like being able to choose what school you go to. More and more frequently, students are able to choose their high schools. This is increasingly the case as more people are attending private schools and even public schools are beginning to work to attract students by developing magnet programs, charter programs, or even just a specialized academic focus.

You may have a wide range of possible issues to consider when choosing a school, including whether they have the academic and extracurricular programing that will help you further your education, whether there is a diverse student body that will expand your understanding of what it means to be a person, and more practical issues like whether it is financially or logistically accessible to you. As a trans or nonbinary person, however, you will need to spend additional time considering whether a school will offer a chance

I did not come out to my friends and peers until high school, the onset of my transition occurring at the start of my sophomore year. During that time I still wasn't ready to tell people what I was, rather I just let them call me "she" and transitioned with my appearance. Around the middle of that same year, I was able to explain myself to a couple of close

peers. Those peers were kind enough to respect my new name and my pronouns, which lead to other people doing the same. My junior year everybody knew what to call me, and I was more able to explain myself to new people or teachers. Then around the middle of my junior year, I moved away from my hometown and went to another school where who I am was what they initially saw. Although I did miss my old school, it was nice to be in a place where I was only known as a man.

Danny

to have more people on your team or if there will be fewer people on your team. You can go through the same steps outlined in the previous section, even if you aren't attending a school yet. The information you find has the potential to make a substantial difference during your years of high school. If you have the opportunity, choose a school where lots of people will be on your team. There are enough hardships that happen to everyone in high school to choose an environment that is not inherently welcoming.

The same applies to choosing what you will do after high school. While some people will attend a college based primarily on its location or cost (like attending the local community college, for example), most people have a greater degree of choice around what happens after they receive their high school degree than the choices they had prior to receiving their high school degree. When this choice includes a school, whether it is a trade school or a college, you definitely have the option to investigate the environment and make sure it is one that will be as welcoming and inclusive as possible.

In Your School

You will find your school's ecosystem is made up of certain categories of people. Each category will require its own sort of attention and engagement.

Administration

Administrators are their own breed. These are people who run the school (the principal, assistant principals, program directors, etc.) and the school district (the superintendent, vice superintendent, etc.). In general, you will find that administrators want to adhere to the school, district, and state rules, policies, and laws. This is their role in the school ecosystem. Sometimes administrators do this to the detriment of the students and the programs they are running. The good administrators, of course, don't do this. Instead, they use their power and control of the environment to set an example and create a culture that is built for maximizing every student's learning capacity—which requires that students feel comfortable and welcomed.

When you find yourself needing to engage with administrators, do what you can to find out where they fall on the spectrum of being welcoming versus being bigoted around gender identity.

Take an advocate with you to these meetings whenever possible. This may be your parent, but if your parent is either not available or not someone who you would consider an advocate, you might ask another school employee like a teacher or a counselor, someone from your local LGBTQ+ center, or another trusted adult to join you.

Meetings with school administrators often have the potential to substantially impact you, your education, and even the educational system in general. Going into any meeting prepared will allow for you to feel comfortable and for the most positive outcome.

Policies

Policies definitely set the tone for your school experience. As referenced above, they impact everything from bathrooms to the ways administrators interact with you. You'll find that policies come from all kinds of unexpected places, depending on the educational structure of your state, school district, and school. You'll need to look up the specific policies in your location. Here are the topics that you'll want to investigate:

- **Bathroom policies**—Which bathrooms can you use? Ideally this policy will state that you will use the bathroom and locker room according to your gender identity.

- **Bullying**—Is there recognition that bullying because of your gender identity is a kind of gender bullying? Ideally, yes! Schools should recognize the increased issues associated with targeted bullying in the same way hate crimes are acknowledged as targeted violence.

- **Confidentiality**—Is the school required to call your parents if you come out as trans or nonbinary at school? Ideally, no! This should be something you have control over.

- **Gender markers**—Can the school change your gender marker on your file? Ideally, yes!

- **Pronouns**—Can the school use your correct pronouns? Ideally, yes!

- **Sports policies**—Which sports teams are you allowed to be on? Ideally, this policy will state that you will play on the sports teams in alignment with your gender identity.

You have two options when it comes to policies: deal with them as they are or try and change them. Neither of these options are easy if the policies are problematic. How much support you have at home will probably determine which choice you make. Chapter 9 has more information on what to do if you run into obstacles in your fight for change.

Bathrooms and Locker Rooms

These spaces, along with other single-gender spaces, can be the most traumatizing of all the school environments. They are, themselves, a force to be reckoned with. There are policies at all levels that you may need to know about related to bathrooms. Your state, school district, and school may all have something to say about which bathrooms they think you should or shouldn't be using. It's important to know about these official opinions even if you don't agree with or appreciate what they have to say. Understanding and advocating for your rights around single-gender spaces can give you access to spaces that are yours.

If your school is unsure about what to do about single-gender spaces, you can refer the necessary people to the resources at the end of this chapter as well as other specific ones you find through organizations that advocate for trans rights like GLSEN and The National Center for Transgender Equality.

However, if your school (or district or state) is outright hostile, that calls for a different approach. Schools that are hostile are sometimes overtly working against trans inclusion and are sometimes pretending to be inclusive while quietly ignoring inclusive steps. If this is the case, you'll need to work to change policy and probably use the advice in Chapter 9 for support.

My school does not have a single gender-inclusive bathroom. There are two one-room restrooms in a corner of the library, and they are reserved for teachers. When I came out, my plan was just to never use a public restroom again, but that plan fell apart very quickly. One day, I saw another transgender student who was nowhere near passing coming out of one of the faculty restrooms, and I figured that was the way to go. I'm occasionally reprimanded by a teacher who thinks I took so long to "go to the bathroom" because I was actually doing something else or yelled at by the librarian ("Do you have some kind of special permission from the principal to use those restrooms? Use your own!"), but at least I don't have to hold it for 8-10 hours.

Coming out was difficult as well. I came out as a senior, so I had three years worth of classmates, teachers, and various faculty members who already knew me. I had no idea how to come out to my classmates, and I have social anxiety, so I made sure in advance that I would be fine if I lost all of my friends, and planned to tell my teachers on the first day of school, hoping that my peers would follow their lead. Luckily, it worked like a charm and my classmates immediately caught on. (The worst reaction I got was from my Linear Algebra teacher who is always trying to increase the number of girls in her higher-level math classes. Turns out, an AFAB classmate of mine had also come out as transgender, and together we had decreased her number of female students by 50%.) My peers made mistakes every now and then but corrected themselves, and their continued support and friendship encouraged me. It took several months, but I'm finally comfortable enough to come out to past teachers and peers who haven't heard about my transition from others. I feel more comfortable with my identity, regardless of where I'm at in physically transitioning (which is nowhere).

Tai

Family Influence

Your family can have an influence in almost everything you do at school. Whether and how much support your parents offer you as it relates to your gender identity will matter in how you are able to interact with the school. Particularly if you are under 18, the school is likely to look to your parents for guidance on how to respond to your coming out and beyond, like how you will have access to bathrooms, athletic teams, academic approaches, and what respectful language and support looks like.

Friends

Friends are people whose company you enjoy, who you share things with, and with whom you have inside jokes. Your friends are the people who believe you when you tell them who you are, who stand by you, and serve as your advocate when you need one. Having friends at school is a gift and a luxury. They make the good days delightful and the bad days bearable.

Your friends are likely to have questions for you about your gender identity. Some of the questions will be appropriate and you'll feel good about answering them—and some of them will be inappropriate and it will bother you that they asked. Thinking through how to respond to a whole range of questions is something you'll need to do for the rest of your life. How you choose to respond will probably depend on how you're feeling that day, how the question was phrased, who else is around, and a whole host of other things. With your friends, answer as many of their questions as you feel good about—and tell them when what they're asking is not okay.

The most difficult thing about friends and friendship is that during the hardest times you may find the people who you thought were your friends are actually not. If they are not strong enough to stand up for and with you as your advocate, but you are accustomed to having them around, it can be tempting to continue to see them and treat them as your friend. But they are not.

Peers

Peers are the other students at your school who aren't your friends. They're the people you pass in the hallway; that kid you've known since you were five but haven't ever talked with and now it's super awkward because you still don't know their name; the person you were BFFs with two years ago but they haven't talked with you since they stole your boyfriend; your sister's friends; that person who seems cool but you've never gotten around to talking with; and so many more random people. You probably feel ambivalent, or like you don't have strong positive or negative feelings, about most of your peers.

Your peers are likely to ask you as many questions as your friends do—but without as much understanding or kindness as your friends bring. You probably feel like disclosing less to your peers than to your friends, but if you are transitioning in a visible way, your peers will have questions that you will have to face in one way or another. Deciding how much you want to tell peers, and how you want to tell them, will be useful. Use your friends or a therapist as a sounding board for picking a set of standard answers you can use in many situations. Your stock answers may be funny, or not, they may be medical, or not, they may include words like trans that not everyone will necessarily know, or not. All of this will depend on how you usually communicate. Figure out answers that feel natural to you and will be relatively easy to say. Make sure one of your answers is along the lines of "I don't feel comfortable/want to answer that question." Feel free to use this one liberally. You do not have to educate anyone about what it means to be trans, either for you or in general.

Teachers and Other School Staff Members

Teachers and other school staff members (like guidance counselors, librarians, bus drivers, or cafeteria workers) can be a wonderful source of support. Their offices and rooms can offer safe spaces away from the hubbub and clamor of the typical school day. They can act as advocates within the school system for you, for both academic- and gender-based issues. Connecting with teachers and other school staff members is also important to long-term academic success because they provide recommendation letters for colleges, scholarships, and more.

However, the reactions of these adults could span from supportive to ambivalent to problematic. You do not have to share anything with problematic staff. Much like with your peers, they may have questions, and you can choose to talk with them as little or as much as you want. Just because someone is an adult does not mean you owe them any piece of your personal self. You can complete the work and succeed in a class without any connection to the specific teacher or other school staff member.

Karen

My first love was teaching. I particularly loved the relationship between teachers and students and all the ways teachers could support students both in and out of the classroom. Most people go into teaching because they want to help and support young people—there certainly aren't very many other perks that come with the job! All of which is to say, there is usually at least one teacher in every school who will be there for you through all trials, as long as you are able to find and open up to them.

Coming Out at School

Your process of coming out at school depends on a variety of factors. You'll have to consider if your school's climate is open and accepting of trans and nonbinary people, if your friends are likely to be supportive, whether there is a GSA (Gender and Sexuality Alliance) club at your school, and if there are teachers or administrators you can turn to for support.

As you come to a decision about when and how you want to come out at school, revisit Chapter 3 to make sure you're prepared. One of those first steps is making sure you have come to know yourself and feel comfortable with who you know yourself to be. Being certain about your identity is going to help you project a sense of confidence to your friends, peers, teachers, and administrators. You'll also want to weigh the risks and benefits of coming out to make sure you are safe, and also decide what to do when word (inevitably) starts spreading about your coming out.

After you've come out, even if your school is relatively safe, you may still encounter people who aren't supportive. They may use the wrong name and pronouns for you, say mean things about trans and nonbinary people in general or about you in particular, or they may try to get physically violent with you. The best thing you can do to keep yourself safe is to have a plan for what you want to do in these cases to address bullying and harassment.

Kathryn

One of the best indicators of a school's acceptance and support of LGBTQIA+ youth is whether or not it has a Gender and Sexuality Alliance club (a GSA). GSAs are organized student groups, usually led by a teacher, that offer a safe space for youth to come together and talk about their experiences at school, advocate for improvements to the school climate for LGBTQIA+ youth, and educate the student body and teachers about the LGBTQIA+ community.

If your school doesn't have a GSA, you can learn how to start one by visiting the GSA Network's website (http://gsanetwork.org) or GLSEN (http://glsen.org).

Finding Your Path

School is a pathway to some careers and a hope for a future where you have autonomy over your own choices. It also offers connections to adults and friends who can support you and access to information and skills. Attending a school that actively works to meet your needs and supports you may still require work as you educate school staff and help them develop their policies and approaches. Or it may require changing schools. Or waiting a year or two until you are able to do those things. Regardless of how you go about finding your path to learning, you can find the one that works for you. Don't be afraid to know what you want and need and to go after it!

I absolutely despise school. Don't get me wrong, I love learning, but I hate the institution that is the American public high school. I hate the inefficiency, I hate the overcrowding, and if I have to hear one more "You gay bro? No homo, tho," I swear I'm dropping out. To me, school feels like an environment where you just can't win. You can't be yourself, you can't fake your entire personality for four years, and you can't fix anything. And believe me, I've tried all of the above.

I would consider my school moderately dysfunctional, so I've put a good deal of effort into trying to fix it. As the founder and president of my school's Genders and Sexualities Alliance, I have declared a war on homophobia at my school. Progress has been very slow and, honestly, I'm not sure if I've made that much of a difference. Making change is hard, and in an institution that is forced to be neutral, it is even harder. Public institutions' inability and refusal to take a stand against things that are so obviously wrong (homophobia, racism, sexism, etc.) is the most frustrating thing in the world to me.

My existence is not a political statement. Taking steps to protect and support LGBTQ+ students is not forcing your political views on anyone. I am in school just trying to learn and live my life, but it's really hard to do that when I don't feel supported.

E.

Additional Resources

thetransbook.com/link/1601
GLSEN's Transgender Model District Policy
Schools are often wildly under-informed about how to support trans and nonbinary students. For them to support you the way you deserve to be supported, they may need resources. GLSEN is a great place to find those resources.

thetransbook.com/link/1602
National Center for Transgender Equality, Know Your Rights: Schools
And, of course, you need information for yourself on how to manage your interactions with your school.

thetransbook.com/link/1603
The National GSA Network offers help starting and maintaining a Gender and Sexuality Alliance club at your school.

CHAPTER 17

WORK

Transgender and gender-nonbinary people, especially youth, find it difficult to find and keep a job for many reasons. This chapter explores options for finding trans-affirming workplaces, interview advice, and how to deal with workplace discrimination. We also discuss coming out at work and transitioning on the job.

Finding Trans-Affirming Workplaces

No one wants to work or spend time in a place that doesn't accept them or treat them well. Sometimes you won't have a choice because you need money and your comfort must be a secondary consideration. But if you have the ability to take time and find trans-affirming places to work, you can earn money and feel reasonably comfortable while you do it.

There are several ways to find trans-affirming workplaces including:

- **Personal experience**—Maybe you already visit places that are trans-affirming, like coffee shops or bookstores. If they're hiring, get your application in! Not only do you know you're likely to be more comfortable, but you'll also get to work in a place where you already enjoy spending time.

- **Word of mouth and social media**—Ask your friends and connections online for recommendations of places to work. It's best to ask them if they have personally worked there or if they know someone who has. If you have the time, reach out and ask the person about their experience, so you get a fuller picture of what you can expect at work.

- **LGBTQIA+ Chambers of Commerce**—Chambers of Commerce are organizations that promote the interests of businesses in a given geographic area. While a generic Chamber of Commerce might help in your job search, be sure to see if there is an LGBTQIA+ Chamber of Commerce in your area. If they have a membership directory, you can reach out to those companies to see what job openings they have. Be careful though: just because a company is owned by a lesbian, gay, or bisexual person who is friendly to other LGB people, they may not be friendly to trans or nonbinary people.

- **Job sites that list LGBTQIA+ friendly employers**—Job search sites are increasingly adding the ability for companies to promote their willingness to hire LGBTQIA+ people and, in turn, making it easier for transgender and gender-nonbinary people to search for and apply for jobs at these companies.

- **If you are old enough, you might be interested in and able to get a job at an LGBTQIA+ bar or sex shop.** These aren't jobs for everyone, but they do offer a chance to be more integrated into the community and meet other LGBTQIA+ adults.

Applying and Interviewing for Jobs

Interviewing for a job can be stressful, especially if you haven't done it before. There are thousands of resources online that can give you advice about the actual interview process, but there are some things specific to trans and nonbinary people that are important to think about too and will vary based on where you're at in your transition.

- Contact the company you'd like to work for ahead of time to anonymously request information about their openness and willingness to interview and hire trans and nonbinary people. This could save you from a potentially embarrassing or dangerous interaction in an unfamiliar environment.

- Reach out to local LGBTQIA+ organizations to see if they have interview preparation programs or to see if they will connect you with a mentor to help you get ready for your interview. You can also see if the career center at your school offers support to trans and nonbinary people applying for jobs.

- It's okay to do what you need to do to get a job—even if that means expressing your gender identity in a way that isn't comfortable or authentic to you. Sometimes you just need a job and know the only way to get one is conforming to what other people think you should be. No job has to be forever. You can keep looking for other places to work where you can dress, act, and be yourself!

Trans-Friendly Companies

The HRC Corporate Equality Index rates companies on how well they treat LGBTQIA+ employees. Listed below are several well-known companies that offer protections and benefits specifically for trans, nonbinary, and queer people.

Airbnb	Hallmark	Office Depot
American Eagle	Hilton Hotels	PepsiCo
Apple	Home Depot	PetSmart
AT&T	Hyatt Hotels	Southwest Airlines
Barnes & Noble	IBM	Sprint
Ben & Jerry's	IKEA	Staples
Best Buy	Indeed	Starbucks
Crate and Barrel	J.C. Penney	Target
CVS	Kohl's	Under Armour
Dollar General	Levi Strauss & Co.	UPS
FedEx	Macy's	Verizon
GameStop	Netflix	Wal-Mart
Gap	Nike	Walt Disney Co.
Google	Nordstrom	

While these companies all received a perfect score on the 2018 Corporate Equality Index, that doesn't mean every LGBTQIA+ person will have a positive experience working for them. A company can make supportive policies, but it's up to the people that work there to respect, support, and implement these policies fairly over time and ensure the company's culture is always working to improve equality for everyone that works there.

- When applying for a job, you will often be asked to provide references saying what a good worker you are. If you are applying as yourself, you will need to provide references from people who know and use your name and pronouns correctly. If you are applying using your deadname and sex assigned at birth, your references will need to use that name and pronouns correctly. Be sure the people who you are asking to be references will match their information to the needs of the application (either because that is the only way they know you or because you have been explicit in telling them).

Karen

Interviewing for a job can be hard under any circumstance. You've generally made it clear that you're interested in doing this thing—and the interview can feel like the moment when you're being judged as good enough or not. This is particularly true if you're a teenager and you're applying for a job where the manager isn't particularly thrilled to be managing teenagers.

What most people don't think about when they're getting ready for a job interview is that you're interviewing them just as much as they're interviewing you. While you might need to accept any job that's offered to you for financial reasons—you might not have to.

If you're applying at a few different places. For example, you might end up in a position where you will need to choose which one is the best fit. And what a great position to be in! Ask the interviewer questions that would help you make that decision.

Interviewers usually really like it when people being interviewed ask them questions too. It shows you're taking an interest, and that if you accept the job, you'll have a deeper understanding of what you'll be doing and hopefully enjoy doing. So dive into interviews with questions of your own! You'll be better informed and you'll have impressed the interviewer all at the same time.

I got my first job in March of 2018. I started working for a local church as a theatre technician, running lights and stage management for them and setting up their band. The thing about theatre tech, especially my school's program, which is where we get hired from, is that it's a primarily cis male dominated industry. There are only around seven active women in the program, and only about five LGBT people besides me. So, working in that  kind of environment for so long kept me from coming out for a while. I didn't come out as trans until late October of 2018. Overall, my friends, coworkers, and my bosses were chill about the entire affair. Well, minus the fact that all my bosses sort of guilt tripped me by saying "Why didn't you tell me sooner?" as if I don't live in Texas and am surrounded by white conservatives most of the time. It was a weird shift, since I didn't have some grandiose moment where I told the whole department. People just sort of found out over a period of time, and I had to answer a few questions about whether or not I was "planning" on growing a penis. By the way, don't ask a trans person that, especially not while you're at work in front of a bunch of Christians just trying to go to church. In my personal experience, however, being trans at work is more awkward than anything.

Luka

One of the big things you may be wondering, curious, or nervous about is how you should present yourself in an interview. There is something to be said for "dressing for the job you want," which means dressing nicely in clean, pressed clothes and having a well-groomed appearance. Where this can be uncomfortable is if you aren't sure if you should go to your interview as yourself. There's no single rule of thumb that can guide you, you'll have to make that determination on your own or in collaboration with your parents, friends, or other trusted adults. You'll have to weigh your need for the job against your need to be seen, accepted, and acknowledged as your true self at work. But never forget you deserve to work in a place that is accepting of you and will defend you from discrimination from your supervisor, coworkers, and customers.

Coming Out at Work

When planning to come out at work, you'll need to do some assessing of the company climate before taking any steps. If you're at a larger company, it might be likely that they have policies and procedures in place for when employees come out. If you're at a smaller company, you may have to do more of your own advocating for what you need.

If there is a Human Resources (HR) department where you work, it's best to start there. In larger companies, this is the department you probably worked closely with when you started your job. If you're not sure if your company has an HR department, ask your supervisor or coworkers or check the employee manual. The HR department may have previous experience helping people navigate coming out at work. They can also be an advocate to you when dealing with less-than-enthusiastic coworkers and colleagues who have an issue with your coming out. If there's not an HR department, test the waters by coming out to a coworker you're close and friendly with. It's best to have folks on your side if you're going to come out company-wide.

You can also come out by writing a letter to your supervisor or another person in leadership at your company. This isn't the same kind of letter you would write to a close friend or family member; this letter is more factual and less emotional in nature (check out the sample letter). While it might seem weird to have that kind of thing in writing, it can be helpful to have documentation if coming out gets you fired. You might need this documentation if you're able to file a complaint or report about your mistreatment.

Your Coming Out at Work Letter

Often, the first step to transitioning at work is to let your company know you are transgender, what your name and pronouns are, and your requests about how they'll handle everything. Sometimes you'll feel safe and comfortable enough at work to do this in a conversation, but you might be in a situation where coming out in a letter is more appropriate.

The sample letter on the next page is just a place to start. Modify it to fit your exact circumstances but keep it professional and factual[1].

Kathryn

I'm lucky to work at an LGBTQIA+ youth center where we are eager and willing to help our employees transition on the job. I actually oversee most of our Human Resources, so I know first-hand what goes into a workplace transition.

One of the things to keep in mind if you come out and transition on the job is that your company (if they're accepting and not awful) will reproduce all sorts of things with your name (and hopefully pronouns) on them. This means they might need to make you a new name tag, print new business cards, set up new accounts for email and other systems, update the website, and all sorts of other things because your name is in so many places.

Because of this, it's important to be relatively certain about the name and pronouns you want to use before asking the company to start that process. Of course, you can come out before you are ready to change all of that information and it's always your right to change your name and pronouns to reflect who you know yourself to be; but it's going to frustrate even the most accepting workplace if you ask for your name to be changed two weeks after they've gone through changing your name already in all of the places. It can also make it harder for other transgender and gender-nonbinary people at your company to get their names updated in the future.

---

1. This is actually a modification of the letter I sent to the MBA program staff when it was time to come out.

Dear <Person's name[2]>,

I am writing to tell you about a matter that is very personal but will result in some changes at work.

You may have noticed over the time we've worked together that <what they may have noticed about your appearance, voice, mannerisms, etc.>. Now it's time to explain what's been going on.

I am <gender identity>. I was born this way. I have had these feelings, a longing to be seen this way, all of my life. I kept those feelings hidden. Not surprisingly, my discomfort and anxiety only increased, and so I began the process of sorting things out.

Outside of work, I have been living as a <woman/man/nonbinary person> for several years. My family and close friends call me <First name>, and I am in the process of having my name legally changed to <Full name>[3].

As part of my transition at work, I am requesting that my name and gender marker be updated in my employment paperwork and all of my identifying documents and accounts. I would also like your assistance in developing a plan for telling my coworkers about this change. It is my hope to begin presenting and identifying as myself at work on <date>, and that you will help me if I encounter any resistance. I'm very pleased to be able to take this step toward personal wholeness while remaining a part of <company name>.

This change will not affect my ability to participate at work or complete my projects. In fact, I may be less distracted when I am no longer consumed with hiding in plain sight. Also, as I enjoy being myself more, you may find me more enjoyable to be around.

You may not understand the life changes I'm undertaking. I would be happy to answer your questions or direct you to additional information.

Respectfully,

<Full Name>
(formerly <old name>)

---

2. This is the name of your supervisor or person in HR that you'll be working with.
3. Of course, if you're not doing this outside of work, change it!

I often wonder what I'm going to be when I grow up. I want to be important, I want to be powerful and respected, I want to help people, and, of course, I want to make money. I know people say you should always do work you love, but I don't think that's always true. Sure, a career I enjoy and am invested in is the end goal, but right now, I'm just trying to get this bread so I can make it through college. Even once I'm able to get a real job, I don't know if I'll necessarily be able to do work I love right off the bat. Happiness in life is important, but it's more important to ensure I have a life, so that might mean just getting a job where I can make enough money to have a place to live, be able to feed myself, get healthcare and transportation, and save some money, because things happen and, when they do, I want to ensure I can continue to support myself until whatever crisis happens is averted.

All that said, though, it's still so, so important to find enjoyment in life. Even if I can't get a job I love now or in the future, I hope I can still find time to do things that make me happy. I am a multifaceted, interesting person, and I want my activities to reflect that.

E.

I have worked in a couple of physics labs, which is interesting considering that physics has one of the highest gender gaps in existence. In one lab I worked in, I was surprised to learn that there was a single girl working somewhere on the same floor as me. I asked the program coordinator to make my name badge using my preferred name and promptly stuck a neon green and orange "He/ Him" pin to it. If I thought I couldn't have been  more clear, I was wrong. Every lab mate I ever heard speak of or to me used she/her pronouns. I wore a chest binder under my father's bulky sweatshirts with jeans every day and spoke in the deepest voice I could muster. I didn't know what I was doing wrong, and I didn't have the confidence to correct anyone. Looking back, I can see why people immersed in academia--especially in a field less than 20% female— wouldn't be aware of gender issues (in my final week, a program coordinator told me she thought my pin referred to God), and I could have definitely made more of an effort to explain to them my situation. It's no fun that we have to explain ourselves and fight to be acknowledged in spaces that should have room for everyone, and we don't exist to be educators, but even a little bit of introduction can go a long way. At my workplaces, I only explicitly came out to the program coordinator, but I made the mistake of not taking her up on her offer to clarify my situation to my advisor and coworkers. The workplace is never easy, but it really helps to find your allies and make good use of them! It's easy to feel shy about asking for things that others don't need—we stand out enough without special requests—but we also have struggles that others aren't at all familiar with, and it's important to ask for what we need.

Transitioning on the Job

Just like coming out, it's best to start by approaching the Human Resources department where you work, if you have one. They may have a standard procedure, but don't be afraid to ask for a different procedure if that's what you need. Just because they've handled one trans person's transition one way doesn't mean that is the way you need or want things done.

If you're in a smaller organization, work with your manager or supervisor to put together a plan and timeline for your transition on the job. You can reach out to local LGBTQIA+ organizations to see what help they can provide to you and your company to make your transition at work as easy as possible.

Dealing With Discrimination at Work

Even if you work at a company that embraces and supports trans and nonbinary people, that doesn't mean everyone in the company is going to be accepting about you and your identity. It can be extremely difficult to have a supervisor or coworkers who are not accepting or are outright hostile about your being trans or nonbinary.

No matter the size of the company you work in, it's important to understand the policies and procedures they have for dealing with workplace discrimination and whether LGBTQIA+ people are specifically mentioned. It is also critical to know if the state or city you work in has laws protecting LGBTQIA+ people from discrimination and harassment in the workplace.

If you are experiencing discrimination at work, it's best to report it to the Human Resources department. If your company doesn't have a Human Resources department, then report the discrimination to your supervisor or some other person in leadership that you think will be supportive and help you stop the problem.

And in the case that you can't get the discrimination to stop, or you aren't hired or promoted because you are trans or nonbinary, or you're fired because of your identity, you can pursue legal action. There's more information and resources in Chapter 9 in this situation.

Do What You Love

It's important to find work you feel passionately about, but it's equally important to work in a place that loves you back. You'll be giving a significant amount of your time to the place you work in return for money (and hopefully fulfillment, learning, and advancement opportunities). Your time is a valuable resource and you must choose wisely where you invest it. And, if the investment turns out not to be a good one, you have every right to take your investment somewhere else, to a place that will receive it with gratitude and help you grow and become even more yourself.

Additional Resources

thetransbook.com/link/1701
The National Center for Transgender Equality has an informative collection of "know your rights" resources, especially around employment and work.

thetransbook.com/link/1702
The Transgender Law Center also has a "know your rights" resource about employment. You might be noticing a theme—that it's critical that you know the laws and your rights to be treated with dignity and respect at work and how to combat discrimination if you experience it.

thetransbook.com/link/1703
Out and Equal is an organization that works to ensure workplace equality for LGBTQIA+ people around the world. They offer resources for companies specifically around welcoming and treating trans and nonbinary people with respect and compassion.

thetransbook.com/link/1704
Lambda Legal provides resources for LGBTQIA+ people to help them understand their employment rights and fight employment discrimination.

CHAPTER 18

SPIRITUALITY AND FAITH

Transgender and nonbinary people are often rejected by their faith communities, but this doesn't mean you have to choose between your identity and your spirituality. Of course, it's also possible spirituality or religion is not important to you, and that's okay too! It doesn't matter how you choose to go about understanding yourself and your place in this world and universe, just as long as you do it in a way that feels authentic to you.

You Deserve to Be Loved

Everyone who wants a spiritual practice to turn to or a faith community to rely on deserves one that is welcoming and safe. Unfortunately, spiritual and religious rejection is all too real for transgender and nonbinary people. This rejection often stems from church leaders selectively interpreting their holy books and philosophical documents in a way that suits their narrow human understanding of what is right and good in the world (and what is wrong and bad in the world).

Any religion, spirituality, or other practice that doesn't love, acknowledge, and accept you for who you are doesn't deserve to have you. If you find yourself in a community that isn't accepting, there are a few other options to explore:

- Search out other faith communities with a reputation for being accepting of transgender and nonbinary people.
- Self-study or join a small study group to explore holy books or other philosophical documents that are important and speak to you.
- Listen to spiritual podcasts.
- Join online groups focused on an accepting approach to spirituality.

Karen

The church I was raised in has been welcoming and inclusive of people who are LGBTQ+ for far longer than it's been cool to do so. One of my mother's favorite stories of me was, at the age of four, having a screaming argument with another child because I believed two women could get married. (They definitely could not at the time.) I've never been part of a church that didn't include and love trans and gender-nonconforming members. There are churches out there where, if this is important to you, you can find a home.

In the Beginning . . .

In many of the world's religions, and especially in Abrahamic traditions, there is a story about the origins of humanity that revolve around the first man and first woman. In Judaism and Christianity, these figures are known as Adam and Eve.

Sometimes, people of faith will hold up the story of Adam and Eve to justify their transphobic views by saying that God only created male and female and nothing in-between. We think this is a terribly short-sighted approach to things, especially when you consider that in these traditions, Eve was made from Adam's rib.

God is life.

God is a Texas winter day, cool, crisp air surrounding you as the sun shines warmly on your face.

God is the bone you could see the day you scraped all the skin off of your knee skating too fast down that hill.

God is the most beautiful girl you've ever seen, the one who you will swear on your life smiled at you in the Walmart at 3AM last Thursday.

God is the boy you thought you loved who laughed louder than you've ever heard anyone laugh on the day you cut your hair.

God is that job you applied for even though you are hilariously underqualified because it would be perfect.

God is all there is and all there isn't.

God is leaving your house and going back in to double-check that you turned the oven off, just in case.

God is Pedro's Pizza Parlor on 34th and Main, the only restaurant that has been open for over 100 years, and has never closed, not once.

God is the woman you married because you realized one day you couldn't imagine living without her.

God is the embrace of a loving mother who has been with you through everything, through all the mistakes and all the successes.

God is utter perfection.

But perfection doesn't exist in my world.

My world is an Arctic winter day, bitter, sharp wind surrounding me with no relief and no sun to be found.

So why God?

Why should God wish to exist here, in the barren plains of my existence?

To subject itself to purple, permanently numb fingers in exchange for what?

In exchange for the sight of polar bears so thin it looks like their skin is four sizes too big for them?

In exchange for frigid pain and no hope for improvement?

I will never have God, because God doesn't exist for people like me.

E.

This sounds an awful lot like cloning, which would mean that Eve has XY chromosomes, which would have made Eve a trans woman.

Now, is it our place to assert that Eve was trans? No. It's based on our interpretation, just as others interpret holy texts to say a whole bunch of things to support their specific positions. If these same people who use literal interpretations of the Bible to denounce transness did the same with other parts of their religious books, they wouldn't wear polyester or eat shrimp.

What's most important is to read the texts that are important to you and see what they tell you about the world, humanity, and how you might try to live your life. Your interpretation is what counts, not anyone else's.

Kathryn

It took me a long time to find a spiritual practice and philosophical texts that worked for me. I was raised without religion until the age of 10 when my family started going to a Methodist church. It wasn't bad, but I didn't find anything there that spoke to me. I left religion again when I got to college and returned to a spiritual practice when I joined a Center for Spiritual Living, a practice based on the practices of Science of Mind (not to be confused with Scientology). There I found a spiritual tradition that spoke deeply to me, connected me to my soul and a deeper understanding of my place in the universe.

I hope you will take your time and find a practice that works for you, if that's what you want. In the meantime, don't be afraid to point it out when people are being hypocritical. If they get mad at you, tell them I gave you permission to tell them to knock off their nonsense.

When Faith and Family Collide

When combined, family and faith can be really difficult to navigate. Maybe your family has been going to the same unaccepting church for years, but they don't want to leave because they like the people. Or maybe you have a few family members who have different religious beliefs from your own, ones that say your identity isn't valid or important.

Religion has always been a very prominent part of my life. I was born to a Roman Catholic family. Although I am presently agnostic, there was a time when I used to rely on the same faith as my family. Ironically when I was questioning my sexuality was when my faith was most sturdy. As a pre-teen, it was nerve-racking to think I could be anything other than what my parents wanted me to be. I decided to submerge myself in the church, believing that doing so could change me; make me into what I thought was normal. So I let it overwhelm my life, and everything I did was for the church. I harshly criticized anything that went against the church's beliefs. Looking back at it, what we used to do is strange; the way we talked about ourselves, how we talked about outsiders; the guilt of my discovery overwhelmed me. With time, all the feelings I had bottled up overflowed. I became angry. With the church  as well as my parents. So I distanced myself from both. That distance allowed me to discover who I really was, and how my transition also affected them. As for the church, I can understand how a message of peace and unconditional love can be comforting, especially since I had once wrapped myself within that comfort. Even with my negative experiences, I can say that I don't hate the people of my past, rather I want to understand them and respect them. They taught me empathy, and without it, I most likely would have lived a life full of anger and confusion. They brought me peace of mind.

Danny

I was raised nonreligious, but I've always been interested in religion. As I got older, I became interested in learning more about it and trying to join a faith community, but it became difficult as I realized I was LGBTQ+. I've made so many compromises in my life, giving up so many parts of myself just to be accepted, when I came out I decided I wouldn't do that with religion. I wouldn't choose religion over myself, and I would only join a faith community that respected and supported me. I believe that all the religions are true, so that's not the problem, but it's a matter of finding the place with the right culture of respect, and I haven't found that yet. However, I'm privileged in a way that very few of us are. Many of my LGBTQ+ friends have been told from a young age that their God or religion doesn't accept those who deviate from the norm, and their only exposure to the idea of gender and sexual diversity was as an example of those who have been forsaken. Granted, not everyone believes this, even within a single community of faith, but when you know that even one person does, I imagine it's easy to feel like you don't belong in the community—or even that there is something intrinsically wrong with you.

Education can also go a long way if your family is experiencing a conflict between their faith and their love for you that might be pushing them toward conversion therapy. The best thing for them is education and resources about what it means to be transgender or nonbinary that speak to them with their faith in mind. The Family Acceptance Project, which we refer to in the references at the end of this chapter, is an amazing resource for parents and families of LGBTQIA+ youth.

Conversion Therapy

Some faith communities believe being LGBTQIA+ is a choice and a sin so they try to change a person's sexual orientation or gender identity to be in line with a cisgender/heterosexual world and faith view. This process is sometimes called "Conversion Therapy," "Reparative Therapy," "Ex-Gay Therapy," or "Psychological Abuse." We will refer to it as Sexual Orientation or Gender Identity Change Efforts (SOCE/GICE) because it's important to call it what it is. But no matter what it's called, the process is the same—it uses a combination of psychological and spiritual approaches to change a person's sexual orientation or gender identity.

SOCE/GICE is based on pseudoscience and is widely condemned by leading organizations like the American Psychological Association and the American Association of Pediatricians. Conversion therapy doesn't work. It doesn't achieve its stated goals and instead actively harms the people who take part in it. People, especially youth, who undergo conversion therapy often suffer from increased dysphoria, depression, anxiety, and suicidal ideation. In fact, the practice is so dangerous, states like California, New Jersey, and Oregon have laws banning such practices. Unfortunately, those laws only apply to licensed professionals who work with minors and sometimes those who would accept money for these "treatments." But these laws are not able to prohibit the practice by spiritual leaders or others who do not seek payment for their "help." Instead, trans and nonbinary youth should have access to affirming mental health care and therapy that helps them understand themselves and better navigate the world around them.

One of the first things I did after I came out was find an open and affirming church. Open and affirming means that the faith community is open to anyone of any background and is accepting of anyone regardless of race, sex, gender, or sexuality. My parents took me to an open and affirming church when I was really young. My mom was raised going to open and affirming Christian churches, so it wasn't too much of a change to ask for from her. My dad went to a different type of church and the LGBT community wasn't too kindly accepted. Learning your right fit for an accepting faith community can be hard. When I first came out, I was going to a church that didn't really respect LGBT identifying individuals and I couldn't come out there due to feeling unsafe. I had to masquerade around as a girl under my dead name. About a year or two later, when I moved where I live now, I found the right church for me. I go to United Christian Church and it is the most accepting and open church I've been to. Not only is it trans friendly, but it is accepting of anyone of any background, race, or religion. During our church lock-ins and camps, they even let trans people room with the group of people who share the gender they identify with rather than rooming by assigned gender. Meaning, I got to sleep in the cabins and rooms with other guys since I am one.

Johnny

There are some things you can do if someone is suggesting you should go through SOCE/GICE, or if your parents or church are pressuring you into it. Do some research by exploring the resources at the end of this chapter. There are many other perspectives and beliefs about what major religions and spiritual texts say about transgender and nonbinary people. Study these and pick the ones that resonate most with you. Develop your own talking points to counter people's negative and hurtful opinions with positive and helpful facts.

What to Do If You Can't Get Out

You might be part of a family that forces you to go to church. Sometimes they want you to go because they think it will fix you. This will be one of the most difficult things you can experience; being told that not only your family but your faith community and your god don't love and accept you.

Sometimes it is possible to convince your family to let you attend a different kind of faith service or study as part of another denomination. Other times, you might be able to get out of going to church by having a job or other academic responsibilities, especially if your family values these highly as well. Sometimes you won't be able to get out. If that's the case, you will have to do your best to hold on and remember that your identity is valid.

Additional Resources

thetransbook.com/link/1801
The Family Acceptance Project

thetransbook.com/link/1802
This website provides a centralized place for trans and nonbinary people to find LGBTQIA+ affirming spirituality resources, news, events, and inspiration.

thetransbook.com/link/1803
Queer Theology provides resources for LGBTQIA+ Christians to help with everything from answering the question "What does the Bible say?" to finding encouragement when they're feeling tested by their faith.

 thetransbook.com/link/1804
Freed Hearts helps parents of conservative religious backgrounds come to understand and accept their LGBTQIA+ children, and helps LGBTQIA+ people heal from religious persecution.

 thetransbook.com/link/1805
The Human Empathy Project fosters empathetic connection around matters of Christian faith, gender, and sexual diversity through free confidential consultations and resources.

Dictionary

These are words that are useful for everyone to know and be able to use fluently in discussions about gender. Some of this language may be unfamiliar to you, particularly because it evolves quickly. Some of this language will be familiar to you, but you may not know specific definitions to use if someone asks what exactly a word means. Some of these words are not appropriate to use, and the details of why are explained. It's also important to remember that, because the language is changing quickly, people may have different definitions for the same words. It's more important to understand what someone means and that you both define a certain word in a certain way.

This dictionary is reprinted from UNHUSHED. Up-to-date versions of this dictionary are available for free at www.unhushed.org.

Advocate: A person who is cisgender and works and campaigns for the rights of trans, gender-nonconforming, genderqueer people, and others who identify as a gender minority.

Agender: A person who identifies as not having a gender; or, being without gender.

Ally: A person who is cisgender and who works and campaigns in alliance (note the connection to the word *ally*) with people who are in the gender minority.

Androgynous: A balance of the feminine and the masculine that includes aspects of both.

Bigender: A person who identifies as having two genders.

Biological sex: A complex group of physical factors that are assigned to male, female, and intersex. The preferred term for this is *"sex assigned at birth"* because many people consider *"biological sex"* to be an offensive term at this point.

Bottom surger:y A medical procedure that changes a person's genitals to bring them into alignment with their gender identity. Some transgender people choose to have bottom surgery, some choose not to, but many do not have access to the surgery whether they would choose to have it or not. It is never polite to ask about a person's genitals, regardless of their gender identity.

Butch: A masculine-expressing person; usually refers to a lesbian whose gender roles are typically categorized as masculine.

Cisgender: A person whose sex assigned at birth (typically "female" or "male") is in alignment with their gender identity.

Cissexism: Treating cisgender people as though they have more rights and moral authority compared to people who are gender minorities.

Cis normative: The assumption that cisgender people are normal and those who are gender minorities are not.

Coming out: Commonly understood as the first time that someone discloses their gender identity or sexual orientation, coming out is actually something that gender and sexual minorities do throughout their lifetimes.

Correct gender pronoun (CGP: The pronouns (*she/her/hers, he/him/his, ze/zir/zirs, they/them/theirs*, etc.) that a person feels most comfortable being referred to as. Using a person's CGP is a critical part of being respectful. It may also be referred to as preferred gender pronoun (PGP).

Cross-dresser: A person who wears clothing that is typically assumed to belong to a different gender. Sometimes called a *transvestite*, although this term is not one that is used frequently anymore and some may consider it offensive.

Dead name: The way some transgender people refer to the name they were given at birth. *Deadnaming* refers to calling a trans, nonbinary, gender fluid, or other non-cis person by the name they were given at birth rather than their chosen name.

Desister: A person who identified as transgender as a child but did not continue to identify as trans into adulthood.

Drag king: A person who dresses as and adopts the character of a man to perform a kind of exaggerated masculinity, usually for entertainment purposes.

Drag queen: A person who dresses as and adopts the character of a woman to project a kind of exaggerated femininity, usually for entertainment purposes.

Estrogen: A steroid hormone that is produced by the ovaries and, in lesser amounts, by the adrenal cortex, placenta, and testes. Some transgender people choose to take this hormone so their bodies will be more feminine.

Femme: A feminine-expressing person; usually refers to a lesbian or gay man whose gender roles are typically categorized as feminine.

Gender: A social construct that is often assumed to be aligned with aspects of biological sex, but that is far broader than biological sex. Different cultures have understood gender in dramatically different ways, with some incorporating an understanding of three or more genders.

Gender binary: A categorization of gender as being either male or female rather than a spectrum. This is a harmful understanding of gender for all people because it categorizes them in ways they might not feel comfortable with.

Gender confirmation surgery: A group of medical procedures that changes a person's body to bring it into alignment with their gender identity. Also called *sexual reassignment surgery*; most people prefer the language *gender confirmation surgery*.

Gender dysphoria: When a person's gender identity is in direct conflict with their physical body, causing mild to extreme psychological distress. "Gender dysphoria" is a classification of mental disorder in the *Diagnostic and Statistical Manual of Mental Disorders IV (DSM IV)*.

Gender expression: The way(s) a person shares information about their gender through their hair, makeup, clothes, and other external aspects of their appearance that they have control over.

Gender-fluid: A person who is able to incorporate all genders into their identity and to flow easily between them.

Gender identity: A person's internal sense of how they relate or do not relate to the social constructs their culture aligns with the sex they were assigned at birth.

Gender-nonconforming: When a person's identity does not readily fall into their culture's understanding of what it should be given their sex assigned at birth.

Gender normative: When someone or something falls into the categories that a culture assigns to a specific sex assigned at birth.

Gender norms: The indicators that a culture assigns to specific sex-related biology, primarily including aspects of a person that are unrelated to biology, such as hobbies, personality traits, and academic models of success.

Genderqueer: A gender identity that describes a person who falls outside of the stereotypical "woman" or "man" binary system. This is also an umbrella term that describes many gender identities outside of the gender binary. *Genderqueer* is sometimes shortened to *queer*. This term has historically been used in negative contexts, but has been reclaimed by many who feel it is more descriptive of them and their communities and experiences than LGBTQ+ or GSRD.

Gender, Sexuality, and Relationship Diversity (GSRD: This describes the wide range of identities that are referred to with LGBTQ+, but is far more inclusive of genders and sexualities. By describing the range of identities broadly, it does not leave any identity out accidentally. It also includes relationship diversity, which refers to, for example, people who identify as polyamorous.

Hermaphrodite: An organism that has fully developed male and female reproductive tracts. While this term was historically used to describe intersex individuals, hermaphroditism does not occur in humans and use of this term to describe people is inaccurate and usually considered offensive.

Hormone therapy: A part of transitioning some transgender people choose and are able to access that shifts their balance of hormones to bring them into alignment with their gender identity.

Intersex: A sex assigned at birth, and sometimes discovered after birth, that indicates the presence of attributes associated with both typical males and typical females. Historically, some people used the word *hermaphrodite* to describe people who were intersex, but this is not an appropriate term and is considered offensive by many.

Misgender: Using pronouns or other words that label a person's gender incorrectly. This is often a painful experience for people, including trans and gender-nonconforming people, especially when done by someone who is aware of their gender identity.

Name change: When a person is transitioning, they often choose a new name for themselves. This can be an important part of the transitioning process and should be respected. Asking a transgender person for their "real" name (referring to the name they were given at birth) is offensive.

Niblet: Also sometimes called a nibbling, this is a gender-neutral word to refer to the children of your siblings.

Nonbinary: A gender identification outside of the two-gender, binary system that many cultures recognize. Some people prefer to spell the word "non-binary" and others prefer "non binary."

Nuncle: Also sometimes called auncle, this is a gender-neutral word to refer to the siblings of your parents.

Outing: When a person discloses another person's gender identity (or sexual orientation) without their permission. Sometimes this is done accidentally and sometimes it is done intentionally. It is never okay to out someone.

Pass: When a trans person is accepted in public to be the sex that is in alignment with their gender identity rather than their sex assigned at birth. Sometimes this is a sought-after feature of transitioning, sometimes it is not.

Persister: A person who identified as transgender in childhood through adulthood.

Primary sexual: Parts of the body directly related to reproduction.

Questioning: The experience of considering one's own gender identity as potentially different from the one associated with one's sex assigned at birth.

Secondary sexual characteristics: Nonreproductive-related biological differences between females and males.

Sex assigned at birth: The female or male markers that are bestowed on a baby at the time of birth. Sex assigned at birth is usually determined based on an infant's external genitalia without taking into consideration additional aspects of the infant's biology or eventual gender identity.

T: Short for *testosterone*, which some transgender people choose to take so that their bodies will be more masculine.

Third gender: A gender identity that is neither woman nor man. In cultures with more than two culturally accepted gender identities, this term would describe those identities.

Top surgery: A medical procedure that changes a person's chest to bring it into alignment with their gender identity. Top surgery can be expensive. Some transgender people choose to have top surgery, some choose not to, but many do not have access to the surgery whether they would choose to have it or not. It is never polite to ask about a person's surgical history, regardless of their gender identity.

Transgender: A person whose gender identity does not match the culturally assumed gender identity associated with their sex assigned at birth. Sometimes called *transsexual*, although this term is not in common use and some may find it offensive.

Transitioning: A series of steps that transgender people may or may not choose to take toward shaping their physical bodies to be more in alignment with the cultural expectation associated with their gender identity. Hormone therapy and surgery are examples of steps that some people have access to during transitioning. Some people may choose to transition without incorporating either surgery or hormones into their biology. Rather, they shift their gender expression so that it is in alignment with their gender identity.

Two-spirit: A third-gender marker that is used in Native American communities to describe a range of experiences outside of cisgender and heterosexual. It is not appropriate for people outside of these communities to use this term.

Bibliography

Chapter 1 — What Is Gender?

California Legislature. (2018). *SCR-110 Sex characteristics* (Senate Concurrent Resolution No. 110). Retrieved from http://leginfo. legislature.ca.gov/faces/billTextClient.xhtml?bill_ id=201720180SCR110

Nonbinary Wiki. (n.d.). *Gender-variant identities worldwide.* Retrieved from https://nonbinary.miraheze.org/wiki/Gender-variant_ identities_worldwide

Chapter 2 — Gender Dysphoria

American Psychiatric Association. (n.d.). *Diagnostic and statistical manual of mental disorders (DSM–5).* Retrieved from https://www.psychiatry.org/psychiatrists/practice/dsm

World Health Organization (2016). *International statistical classification of diseases and related health problems (10th revision).* Retrieved from http://apps.who.int/classifications/icd10/browse/2016/en

Chapter 3 — Coming Out

Brill, S., & Kenney, L. (2016). *The transgender teen.* Jersey City: Cleis Press.

Brill, S., & Pepper, R. (2008). *The transgender child: A handbook for families and professionals.* Jersey City: Cleis Press.

Human Rights Campaign Foundation. (2014). Transgender visibility guide: A guide to being you [Brochure]. Author. Retrieved September 2018, from https://www.hrc.org/resources/transgender-visibility-guide

Chapter 4 — Developing Bodies

Rasmussen, A. R., Wohlfahrt-Veje, C., Tefre de Renzy-Martin, K., Hagen, C. P., Tinggaard, J., Mouritsen, A., Mieritz, M. G., & Main, K. M. (2015). Validity of self-assessment of pubertal maturation. *Pediatrics*, 135 (1), 86-93.

The World Professional Association for Transgender Health. (2012). *Standards of care for the health of transsexual, transgender, and gender-noncomforming people.* Retrieved from https://www.wpath. org/publications/soc

Chapter 5 — Reproduction and Having Children

Cocker, C., Hafford-Letchfield, T., Rutter, D., Tinarwo, M., McCormack, K., & Manning, R. (2018) Transgender parenting across the life-course: Findings from a systematic review. In: Social Work and Sexualities International Conference, 11-12 August 2018, University of Montreal, Montreal, Canada.

Stotzer, R. L., Herman, J. L., & Hasenbush, A. (2014). *Transgender parenting: A review of existing research.* UCLA: The Williams Institute.

Chapter 6 — Dismantling the Trans Narrative

Erickson-Schroth, L. (2014). *Trans bodies, trans selves: A resource for the transgender community.* New York, NY: Oxford University Press.

Mock, J. (2017). *Trans in the media: Unlearning the 'trapped' narrative & taking ownership of our bodies.* Retrieved from https://janetmock.com/2012/07/09/josie-romero-dateline-transgender-trapped-body/

Riley Snorton, C. (2017). *Black on both sides: A racial history of trans identity (3rd edition).* Minneapolis, MN: University of Minnesota Press.

Rosskam, J. (2009) *Against a trans narrative* [film]. Retrieved from http://www.vdb.org/titles/against-trans-narrative

Sycamore, M. B. (2006). *Nobody passes: Rejecting the rules of gender and conformity.* Emeryville, CA: Seal Press.

Walker, A. & Lundberg, E. J. P. (2015). *Finding masculinity: Female to male transition in adulthood.* Bronx, NY: Riverdale Avenue Books.

Chapter 7 — Social Transition

Olson, K. R., Durwood, L., DeMeules, M., & McLaughlin, K. (2016). Mental health of transgender children who are supported in their identities. *Pediatrics*, 137. https://dx.doi.org/10.1542/peds.2015-3223

Peitzmeier, S., Gardner, I., Weinand, J., Corbet, A. & Acevedo, J. (2016). Health impact of chest binding among transgender adults: A community-engaged, cross-sectional study. *Culture, Health, & Sexuality, 19.* https://doi.org/10.1080/13691058.2016.1191675.

Sherer, I. (2016). Social transition: Supporting our youngest transgender children. *Pediatrics*, 137. https://pediatrics.aappublications.org/content/137/3/e20154358

Chapter 8 — Medical Transition

LGBTQ Parenting Network. (n.d.) *Surgery: A guide for MTFs.* Retrieved from http://lgbtqpn.ca/wp-content/uploads/woocommerce_uploads/2014/08/Surgery-MTF.pdf

LGBTQ Parenting Network. (n.d.) *Surgery: A guide for FTMs.* Retrieved from http://lgbtqpn.ca/wp-content/uploads/woocommerce_uploads/2014/08/Surgery-FTM.pdf

The World Professional Association for Transgender Health. (2012). *Standards of care for the health of transsexual, transgender, and gender-noncomforming people.* Retrieved from https://www.wpath.org/publications/soc

Chapter 9 — Legal Transition

Lambda Legal (n.d.) *Transgender rights toolkit.* Retrieved from https://www.lambdalegal.org/publications/trans-toolkit

Martell, A. (2017). Legal issues facing transgender and gender-expansive youth. *Michigan Bar Journal.* http://www.michbar.org/file/barjournal/article/documents/pdf4article3272.pdf

National Education Association (2016). *Legal guidance on transgender students' rights.* Retrieved from https://www.nea.org/assets/docs/20184_Transgender%20Guide_v4.pdf

Chapter 10 — Dating

Brooks Tompkins, A. (2014) "There's no chasing involved": Cis/trans relationships, "tranny chasers," and the future of a sex-positive trans politics, *Journal of Homosexuality*, 61, 766-780.

Lenhart, A., Smith, A., & Anderson, M. (2015). *Teens, technology and romantic relationships.* Washington DC: Pew Research Center.

Chapter 11 — Healthy v. Unhealthy Relationships, Consent, Safety, and Other Relationship Buzzwords

Ewing, S. F. & Bryan, A. D. (2016). A question of love and trust? The role of relationship factors in adolescent sexual decision-making. *Journal of Developmental & Behavioral Pediatrics* 36, 628–634. http://dx.doi.org/10.1097/DBP.0000000000000190

Muehlenhard C. L., Humphreys T. P., Jozkowski K. N., & Peterson Z. D. (2016). The complexities of sexual consent among college students: A conceptual and empirical review. *Journal of Sex Research*, 53, 457-87. http://dx.doi.org/10.1080/00224499.2016.1146651.

Schubert, K. (2015). Building a culture of health: Promoting healthy relationships and reducing teen dating violence. *Journal of Adolescent Health*, 56, S3-S4.

Chapter 12 — Relationship and Sexual Violence

Matsuzaka, S. & Koch, D.E. (2018). Trans feminine sexual violence experiences: The intersection of transphobia and misogyny. *Affilia, 34,* 28–47. https://doi.org/10.1177/0886109918790929

Phipp, A., Ringrose, J., Renold, E., & Jackson, C. (2017). Rape culture, lad culture and everyday sexism: Researching, conceptualizing and politicizing new mediations of gender and sexual violence. *Journal of Gender Studies, 27,* 1–8 https://doi.org/10.1080/09589236.201 6.1266792

Chapter 13 — Doing It

Ettner, R., Monstrey, S., & Coleman, E. (2016). *Principles of transgender medicine and surger (2nd edition).* New York, NY: Routledge.

Nikkelen, S. W. C. & Kreukels, B. P. C. (2017). Sexual experiences in transgender people: The role of desire for gender-confirming interventions, psychological well-being, and body satisfaction. *Journal of Sex & Marital Therapy, 44,* 370–381. https://doi.org/10.1080/ 0092623X.2017.1405303

Chapter 14 — Safer Sex

Centers for Disease Control and Prevention. (n.d.). *HIV and transgender people.* Retrieved from https://www.cdc.gov/hiv/group/gender/ transgender/index.html

Johns, M. M., Beltran, O., Armstrong, H. L., Jayne, P. E., & Barrios, L. C. (2018). Protective factors among transgender and gender variant youth: A systematic review by socioecological level. *The Journal of Primary Preventions, 39,* 263–301.

Chapter 15 — Family

Katz-Wise, S. L., Budge, S. L., Orovecz, J. J., Nguyen, B., Nava-Coulter, B., & Thomson, K. (2017). Imagining the future: Perspectives among youth and caregivers in the trans youth family study. *Journal of Counseling Psychology, 64,* 26-40. http://dx.doi.org/10.1037/ cou0000186

Mathews, S. K., Kuper, L., & Lau, M. (2018). Transgender youth and their parents' perceptions of mental health quality at baseline and at one-year follow-up. *Journal of Adolescent Health, 62,* S34–S35. https://doi.org/10.1016/j.jadohealth.2017.11.069

Chapter 16 — School

Goodrich, K. & Barnard, J. (2018). Transgender and gender non-conforming students in schools: one school district's approach for creating safety and respect. *Sex Education, 19,* 212–225.

Meyer, E. J., Tilland Stafford, A., & Lee, A. (2016). Transgender and gender-creative students in PK-12 schools: What we can learn from their teachers. *Teachers College Record, 118.*

Chapter 17 — Work

National Center for Transgender Equality. (2014). *Employment discrimination and transgender people.* Retrieved from https://transequality.org/sites/default/files/docs/kyr/EmploymentKnowYourRights_July2014.pdf

Out & Equal Workplace Advocates. (2015). *Workplace gender identity and transition guidelines.* Retrieved from http://outandequal.org/app/uploads/2016/09/Transition-Guidelines-Full-Edition.pdf

Transgender Law Center. (2016). *Know your rights: Transgender people at work.* Retrieved from http://transgenderlawcenter.org/wp-content/uploads/2012/05/01.28.2016-KYR-Trans-People-at-Work.pdf

Chapter 18 — Spirituality and Faith

American Psychological Association, Task Force on Appropriate Therapeutic Responses to Sexual Orientation. (2009). *Report of the american psychological association task force on appropriate therapeutic responses to sexual orientation.* Retrieved from https://www.apa.org/pi/lgbt/resources/therapeutic-response.pdf

The Williams Institute. (2018). *Conversion Therapy and LGBT Youth.* Retrieved from https://williamsinstitute.law.ucla.edu/wp-content/uploads/Conversion-Therapy-LGBT-Youth-Jan-2018.pdf

UK Council for Psychotherapy. (2014). *Converstion therapy: Consensus statement.* Retrieved from https://www.psychotherapy.org.uk/wp-content/uploads/2016/08/ukcp-conversion-therapy.pdf

Index

ABOUT THE AUTHORS

Kathryn Gonzales, MBA, is the Operations & Programs Director at Out Youth, a Co-Chair of the steering committee for the Central Texas Transgender Health Coalition, the Chair of the board of directors at Haven-Con, and a commissioner on the City of Austin's LGBTQ Quality of Life Commission. Kathryn is always seeking out new ways for youth to share their stories with the world.

Visit www.outyouth.org and follow @thelonestardiva on Twitter.

Karen Rayne, PhD, is the author of *Girl: Love, Sex, Romance and Being You*, which was features in Teen Vogue, on npr.org, and earned a starred review in Publishers Weekly. She is Executive Director of the nonprofit UNIHUSHED, writes comprehensive sexuality materials, and trains professionals internationally. She lives in Austin, TX.

Visit www.karenrayne.com, www.unhushed.org and follow her on Instagram @karenrayne.

ABOUT THE ILLUSTRATORS

Anne Passchier mixes graphic shapes with subtle texture in their illustrations. Originally from The Netherlands, they currently live in Cleveland, Ohio.

Visit http://www.annepasschier.com/.

Nyk Rayne is an illustrator and animator with a BFA from the Art Institute of Houston. She lives in Austin, TX.

Follow @TruncheonM on Twitter.

ABOUT MAGINATION PRESS

Magination Press is the children's book imprint of the American Psychological Association. Through APA's publications, the association shares with the world mental health expertise and psychological knowledge. Magination Press books reach young readers and their parents and caregivers to make navigating life's challenges a little easier. It's the combined power of psychology and literature that makes a Magination Press book special.

Visit www.maginationpress.org.